Physics for the IB Diplor

Paper 1 Multiple Choice

Worked Solutions

ISBN: 9798589009293

Imprint: Independently published

Table of Contents

Introduction

What is paper 1?

Paper 1 for IB Physics HL is a set of 40 multiple-choice questions, to be completed in 1 hour. Each question has 4 options, of which only one is correct. All questions are equally weighted, with one mark for a correct answer and no negative marking for incorrect attempts. From 2016-2019, paper 1 constituted 20% of total marks for HL. In 2021, as there will be no paper 3 (as of 12/2020), paper 1 has an even higher weightage.

Why is paper 1 preparation important?

Paper 1 is widely considered very challenging, even by top candidates. That's why it's crucial for all students to dedicate specific time to tackle paper 1 questions. In addition, there are specific techniques needed to answer paper 1 (see the tips section on page 142 for a complete compilation) that are separate to understanding the syllabus.

What's in this book?

This book is divided into 4 sections:

1. Detailed solutions for every HL paper 1 question (every season and time-zone) from 2016 to 2019 (all released papers of the current syllabus)
2. General paper 1 tips and strategies from the perspective of an examiner
3. IA success strategies (including a thorough checklist) and a sample level-7 IA
4. [Bonus] A sample A-grade EE written by a 45-point student (will be sent by email if you request for it; you can find our email ID on page 170)

Who is this book for?

We expect most candidates who use our book to be familiar with most IB Physics theory (or at least familiar with the theory for the questions you're answering). However, we will always provide you with the equations you need in the answer itself, and a brief description of what it does to jog your memory. This book can't be used in isolation to teach you material from scratch (remember, you shouldn't really be attempting past papers till you have covered the syllabus!).

How to use the multiple-choice worked solutions in this book?

1. Complete the past paper questions you want (this could be a complete paper in examination conditions, part of a paper, or specific questions to tackle a certain topic)
2. Find the answer section for each question in section 1
3. Check the letter-answer on the left column of the worked solutions
   a. If your answer was correct, still skim through our sample solution; we often put shortcuts and other efficient ways to answer the question that you might have missed
   b. If your answer was incorrect, begin to read through our solution. Try to minimise the number of steps you read – ideally, you should only read through the answer until you become 'unstuck' and then go back and try the question again.

1. B Recall that the volume of a sphere, V, given radius r is:

$$V = \frac{4}{3}\pi r^3$$

Similarly, the volume of a cube is s^3.

The general formula for calculating percentage uncertainty for an equation $y = a^n$ is:

$$\frac{\Delta y}{y} = \left| n \frac{\Delta a}{a} \right|$$

(In simple terms, you take the uncertainty in a, multiply by the power and if the result is negative, make it positive)

From here, we need to know the absolute uncertainty of the radius of the sphere and the side length of a cube. These are:

$$u_r = 5 \pm 0.1\text{cm}$$
$$u_s = 10 \pm 0.2\text{cm}$$

We can now calculate the percentage uncertainty for the sphere:

$$3\left(\frac{0.1}{5}\right) \times 100 = 6\%$$

And the cube:

$$3\left(\frac{0.2}{10}\right) \times 100 = 6\%$$

From here we know that the ratio is

$$\frac{6}{6} = 1$$

Which corresponds to **B**.

---

2. A As the person jumps, her velocity increases because of the acceleration due to gravity. As air resistance keeps increasing with speed, and weight remains constant, her velocity begins to increase at a slower rate, until velocity stops increasing (reaching terminal velocity). After she opens the parachute, there is a much greater value of air resistance when compared to the downward weight, and so her velocity begins to decrease until a new terminal velocity is reached. Therefore, this corresponds to diagram **A**.

3. D The weight of the object is acting downwards, there is friction between the block and the slope and there is a normal reaction force acting at 90 degrees. The below diagram shows the scenario:

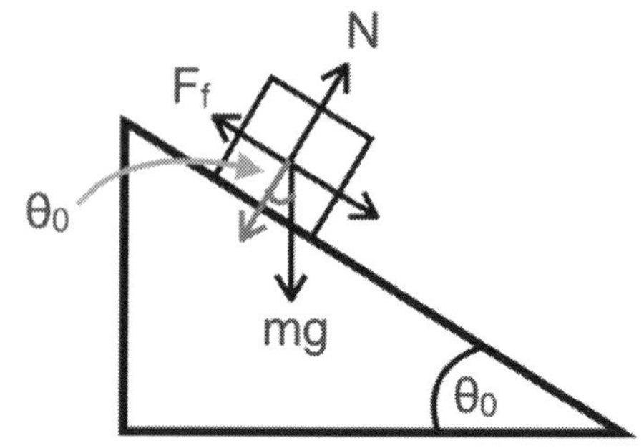

The component of mg that is perpendicular to the plane of the slope is the value of normal reaction:

$$mgcos\theta$$

The component of mg that is parallel to the plane of the slope is equal to the value of frictional force which is

$$\mu_s mgsin\theta$$

Equating the two we have

$$mgcos\theta = \mu_s mgsin\theta$$

Simplifying this, we get

$$\mu_s = \frac{sin\theta}{cos\theta}$$

So, the coefficient of static friction is $tan\theta$ and the normal reaction force is $mgcos\theta$. Therefore, the correct answer is option **D.**

4.A The difference between kinetic energy before and after the collision gives you the loss in KE. So where u is initial velocity and v is final velocity, we have:

$$\frac{1}{2}m(u^2 - v^2)$$

The formula for average force is $\frac{\Delta p}{\Delta t}$ which is also $\frac{m\Delta v}{\Delta t}$.
Since u and v are acting in different directions, we get the average force to be

$$\frac{m(v - (-u))}{T}$$

u is negative of v because they act in different directions and we know that the change in time is T. Therefore, the correct answer is option **A.**

5.D We know that $P = Fv$. From the question, we know that velocity is increasing and, because acceleration is constant while resistive force is increasing, we know that thrust force also increases to overcome the friction. Therefore, the correct answer is **D.**

6.C The formula for work done is $Fscos\theta$ and $F = ma$. Therefore, we know that

$$W = mas$$

We can assume that the direction of force and distance needs to be the same for work to be done so $\theta = 0$. The area under the graph gives the $a \cdot s$ part of the above equation which is just adding the area of a rectangle and a triangle which is 400. Multiplying by the mass with the area gives us 1200J. Therefore, the correct answer is option **C.**

7.B From the question we know that mass is $0.6kg$, the latent heat of fusion if $200KJ/kg$ and the time acting is $40s$. The energy supplied to the substance is obtained by

$$Q = mL$$

And now to get power, which is $\frac{energy}{time}$, we have

$$\frac{Q}{\Delta t} = \frac{mL}{\Delta T}$$

So simply Power is 3 KJ if we substitute the appropriate values into the above equation. Therefore, this is simply 3000J every second which is just 3000W. Therefore, the correct answer is option **B.**

8.A An ideal gas has a high temperature, very low pressure, and a very low density. This is because the model of the ideal gas states that the gas has negligible intermolecular forces of attraction which only happens at the conditions mentioned previously. Therefore, the correct answer is option **A.**

9.B The light passes through two polarizers which are at different angles. When initial intensity, I_0, passes through P, we can find the final intensity using

$$I = I_O \cos^2 \theta$$

This is 0 for the polarizer at 0 degrees for polarizer A.
For a value of $\theta = 45$, the intensity coming from P is half of initial velocity and using that in the equation

$$I = I_O \cos^2 \theta$$

we get $\frac{1}{4}(I_O)$, thus obtaining the answer. Therefore, the correct answer is option **B.**

10.D In a pipe that is open on both sides, there is half of a wave and when there is a pipe that is open on only one side we see one-fourth of a wave. We know the formula

$$c = f\lambda$$

For the first pipe, this is

$$c = f(2L)$$

And the second pipe,

$$c = f(4L')$$

These formulae were obtained by comparing the wavelength of the wave to the length of the pipe by seeing how much of the wave fit into the pipe. We can now see that the ratio

$$\frac{L}{L'} = \frac{1}{2}$$

Therefore, the correct answer is option **D.**

11.D When light moves from an optically rarer medium to optically denser medium we know that the light slows down and so the ray bends towards the normal. In essence, the angle with the normal decreases. The speed of the wave increases, and the frequency remains the same, and for the frequency to remain same we need to wavelength to decrease as $v = f\lambda$. Therefore, the correct answer is option **D.**

12.C The resistance in parallel can be calculated by

$$\frac{1}{R} = \frac{1}{R1} + \frac{1}{R2}$$

The resistance is now 2 ohms when we substitute values. Since the ammeter has a resistance of 1 ohm, the total resistance is 3 ohms. We know that

$V = IR$ and so $R = \frac{V}{I}$ and $I = \frac{V}{R}$

and so, we know that the current through the ammeter is $\frac{6}{3} = 2$. The voltage across the voltmeter can be calculated by finding the current flowing through one resistor ($1A$) and its resistance (4 ohms). Hence, the voltage is $4V$. Thus, the answer is **C.**

13.A For this question, we must use Fleming's left-hand rule and use the formula

$$F = BILsin\theta$$

By applying the left-hand rule, we know that the direction of force is the direction pointing to the one shown in option A and B. Since the angle is 90 degrees, we get

$$F = BIL$$

Therefore, the correct answer is option **A.**

14.D Realize that "the force exerted by the rod on the mass" is the same as the tension between them. Let's go through the 3 main forces present in all centripetal interactions:

1. The centripetal force which is <u>of constant magnitude</u> (as speed doesn't change) and acts towards the centre of the circle
2. The weight force which is also <u>constant</u> and always acts <u>downwards</u>

All other forces must add up in a vector fashion (accounting for direction) to equal centripetal force. This brings us to:

3. The tension force which is the difference between 1 and 2

The difference between centripetal and weight force (i.e., the tension) is smallest when they act in the same direction. This is at the top of the circle and thus, option **D** is the correct answer.

15.C The maximum number of frequencies is simply the number of different transitions between energy levels. This corresponds to the various arrows that can be drawn between them (between the horizontal lines in figure 15.1). Remember that arrows need not necessarily begin at the topmost line!

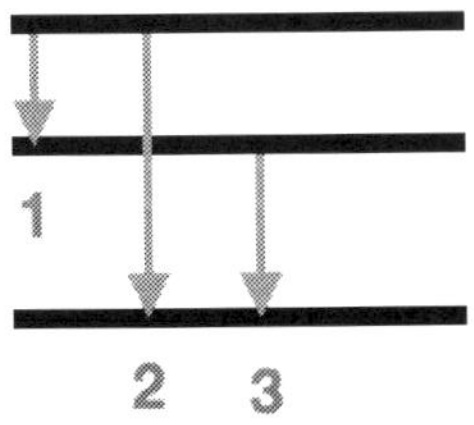

Fig. 15.1, 3 transitions can be made given 3 distinct energy levels

For a larger number of energy levels, such as 5, the maximum number of frequencies can be expressed in this formula (which in mathematics is a general formula for the number of *pairs* that can be formed between *n* elements):

$$N_{max} = \frac{n(n-1)}{2}$$

Here, n is the number of energy levels. For 5 lines, this results in a maximum of **10** frequencies, corresponding to **C**. If you have time at the end, you can always check with arrows on a diagram as well.

16.C **[Memorise]** The four fundamental forces in increasing order of strength are:

Gravitational, Weak, Electromagnetic, Strong

Hence, the answer is **C**

17.A Any atom that holds itself together does so as a result of the balance between the strong nuclear force, to which neutrons contribute, and the repulsive forces between the positively charged protons (which is in fact an electromagnetic force).
As the atom (i.e. proton number) gets larger, a greater number of neutrons than protons are needed to sustain this balance. This is because the range of the strong force is very limited, so more protons between neutrons need even more neutrons to ensure they are all held together. This concept is shown by the upwards curvature on the graph of neutron number against proton number, and corresponds to answer **A.**

18.D Because the solar panels are not 100% efficient, we need to take efficiency into account.

$$\text{efficiency} = \frac{useful\ power\ out}{total\ power\ in}$$

Given that this question asks for the power output of 10 panels, each with 50% efficiency, the equation to be used is deduced:

$useful\ power\ out\ = 10 * 0.5 * (total\ power\ into\ one\ solar\ panel)$

Where total power into one solar panel:

$$I_0 * A$$

$$= 0.25 * 10^3 * 0.4$$

$$= 100W$$

Remember that the intensity is given in kW, which is equal to 1000W.
Combining the two equations gives the useful power output of all 10 solar panels to be $500W$, which is **D.**

Note: The use of the word 'average' in the question may mislead some students into thinking they take the power output of just one solar panel. However, this usage of 'average' refers only to the fact that <u>average</u> intensity is used.

19.B Consider the steps taken to convert the energy in coal into electricity, which is what a coal power station does:

Coal is burned to **heat water,**
which **moves turbines**
which generate **electricity**

From here it's quite straightforward to deduce the energy types contained or represented by each source:

coal > hot water > moving turbines > generated energy
Corresponds to **B:**
chemical > thermal > kinetic > electrical

20.D Let us see what each statement deals with, and use the relevant equation:

I. The temperature in Kelvin

$$T = \frac{2.9 * 10^{-3}}{\lambda_{max}} = 1000$$

II. The energy radiated in one second (which is power, P)

$$P = e\sigma AT^4$$

Because this is a black body, a perfect absorber and radiator of energy, $e = 1$

$$P = (1) * (5{,}67 * 10^{-8}) * (10^3)^4 = 5.67 * 10^4 J$$

III. The body is a perfect absorber

This is shown to be true in statement II

We can therefore see that all statements are true, so the answer is **D.**

21.A The formula for <u>angular</u> frequency is

$$\omega = \frac{2\pi}{T}$$

where T is the time period of the oscillation. This formula does not depend on x_0 while all the other formulae have x_0 in them. Therefore, the correct answer is option **A.**

22.C We know that the angle the ray makes is given by

$$\theta = \frac{\lambda}{b}$$

where λ is the wavelength and b is slit width. We know that b is constant and so as λ increases, θ increases. Therefore, we need a colour with highest wavelength to make the highest width of the central peak. So, the order must read blue (the lowest wavelength), green (higher wavelength than blue but smaller than red, and red (which has highest wavelength). Therefore, the correct answer is option **C.**

23.B The relevant equation here is

$$s = \frac{\lambda D}{d}$$

s is the angular distance between peaks and can be measured on the graph to be 0.01 rad. Therefore,

$$\frac{0.01}{D} = \frac{\lambda}{d}$$

We don't know the value of D, the distance from the slit to the interference pattern, so we have to use some estimation. For λ/d to be 100, D would have to be an absurdly small distance, so we conclude that it has to be 0.01, eliminating options A and C.

We also know that the overall shape of the double-slit interference pattern (discounting the miniature peaks and troughs inside each 'bigger' peak and trough) matches the shape of an equivalent single-slit pattern. We conclude that the effect of single-slit diffraction is still important (non-negligible), making the answer **B.**

24.A We know that the time period of a pendulum is given by

$$T = 2\pi\sqrt{\frac{l}{g}}$$

The mass does not affect the period and so we must only worry about the length. Since the lengths are different, the respective formulae are

$$T = 2\pi\sqrt{\frac{l}{g}} \text{ and } T_{new} = 2\pi\sqrt{\frac{l}{4g}}$$

The latter simplifies to

$$T_{new} = 2\pi\left(\frac{1}{2}\right)\cdot\sqrt{\frac{l}{g}}$$

Which is $T_{new} = \pi\sqrt{\frac{l}{g}}$ and that is clearly half of the initial T that we had. Therefore, the correct answer is option **A.**

25.D We know that the formula we need to use is

$$f' = f\left(\frac{v}{v - u_s}\right)$$

when the training is moving towards the observer and

$$f' = f\left(\frac{v}{v + u_s}\right)$$

when the train is moving away from the observer. Since $v - u_s < v$ we have $f' > f$ and it is the opposite for when the train is moving away so $f' < f$. The only graph from the option that fits these statements is option **D.**

26.B If the charge moves from lower potential to higher potential then it does so by doing work. Moreover, greater the change in potential, higher the work done. And so, by keeping these two points in mind, the greatest work done is when the charge goes from 10V to 30V as there is a difference of 20V and it goes from lower potential to higher potential. Therefore, the correct answer is option **B.**

27.C Because the droplets move at constant velocity, net force is 0. Therefore, gravitational force is equal to the force generated by the electric field, which is given by this equation from section 5.1 of the data booklet:

$$E = \frac{F}{q}$$

From this, we know $F = Eq$. For gravitational force, $F = mg$. Therefore:

$$mg = Eq$$

And therefore,

$$E = \frac{mg}{q}$$

which corresponds to **C**.

28.B Kinetic energy for an orbiting body is given by:

$$\frac{GMm}{2r}$$

While potential energy is given by

$$\frac{-GMm}{r}$$

Therefore, total energy is

$$\frac{GMm}{2r}-\frac{GMm}{r}=-\frac{GMm}{2r}$$

Therefore, kinetic energy is always positive (above the x axis), while total and potential energy are always negative (below the x axis). This is only found in option B and D.

However, in option D, potential energy has a smaller magnitude than total energy (its plot is closer to the x axis). This contradicts our equations, which show that total energy has half the magnitude of potential energy. This leaves **B.**

29.A For emf to be generated, the coil must <u>cut through</u> magnetic field lines. However, throughout the rotation of the coil, it does not cut through the field lines. In other words, flux linkage is always 0 because, at 90°, the coil is parallel to magnetic field lines. As such, as flux linkage is not changing, the emf is 0, which corresponds to option **A.**

30.C We know the formula

$$\varepsilon = BvL$$

where ε is the induced emf. We also know that

$$P=\frac{V^2}{R}$$

Substituting the first equation in the second gives

$$P=\frac{(BvL)^2}{R}=\frac{v^2B^2L^2}{R}$$

Therefore, the answer is option **C.**

31.C We know that

$$P = \frac{1}{2} I_0 V_0$$

where P is the average power, I_0 is peak current and V_0 is peak voltage. Rearranging the first equation gives

$$I_0 = \frac{2P}{V_0}$$

We also know that

$$I_{rms} = \frac{I_0}{\sqrt{2}} = \frac{2P}{V_0} \div \sqrt{2} = \frac{2P}{\sqrt{2} \, . \, V_0} = \frac{\sqrt{2} \, .P}{V_0}$$

Therefore, the answer is option **C**.

32.A The period is 6.3ms and the current is in the shape of a sin curve since this is AC current. Full wave rectifications are meant to <u>reduce</u> the fluctuations that happen in AC current and make it fully positive.

If you draw a graph of the AC current and make peaks in the full-wave rectification graph of all the instances where there is a peak/trough in the AC current graph (with a period of $6.3ms$) you will see that the peaks of these graphs match. The general shape of a full-wave rectification is the ones shown in options A and D, so option **A** is correct because the peaks match the period of AC current which is $6.3ms$.

33.D We know that

$$E = \frac{F}{Q}$$

where E is the electric field. We also know that

$$F = k\frac{Q_1Q_2}{r^2}$$

According to the first equation, E is directly proportional to F and according to the second equation, F is inversely proportional to the square of the distance (r^2)
Thus, it can be concluded that E is also inversely proportional to the square of the distance (r^2)
As the distance between the plates is increased, the magnitude of the electric field between them decreases. We also know that

$$C = \varepsilon\frac{A}{d}$$

where C is the capacitance. From the third equation, we can deduce that the capacitance is inversely proportional to the distance between the plates. Thus, we can conclude that as the distance between the plates increases, the capacitance decreases. And so, the answer is option **D.**

34.C We know that

$$\frac{1}{C_{series}} = \frac{1}{C_1} + \frac{1}{C_2} + \ldots$$

Capacitance of capacitors in series

$$\frac{1}{C_s} = \frac{1}{C} + \frac{1}{C} = \frac{2}{C}$$

$$C_s = \frac{C}{2}$$

We also know that

$$C_{parallel} = C_1 + C_2 + \ldots$$

The two capacitors in series are in parallel with the third capacitor. Hence, the complete capacitance

$$C_p = \frac{C}{2} + C = \frac{3C}{2}$$

which give us option **C** to be the correct answer.

35.B In electron diffraction, electrons behave as waves when diffracted through a slit. Thus, matter behaves as waves, providing evidence for the existence of matter waves. Therefore, the answer is option **B**.

36.D We know that

$$P(r) = |\psi|^2 \Delta V$$

where $P(r)$ is the probability of finding the particle at a distance x, ψ is the amplitude of the wave function and V is the volume.

It can be deduced from the first equation that larger the amplitude of the wave function, higher the probability $P(r)$.

We also know that

$$\Delta x \Delta p \geq \frac{h}{4\pi}$$

where Δx is the uncertainty in the position of the particle and Δp is the uncertainty in the momentum of the particle. It can be deduced from the second equation that smaller the value of Δx, larger the value of Δp. Δx and Δp have an inverse relationship.

The smaller the area under the graph, the region where the particle can be found is relatively well defined and restricted. Hence, the particle will most likely be in the restricted region where the amplitude is high. As a consequence, the uncertainty in position (Δx) is less. In order to find the largest uncertainty in momentum, we have to look for the graph where the area under the curve is the smallest.

So, **D** is the correct answer.

37.B Deviations from Rutherford scattering occur when the α-particle approaches the nucleus so closely that the strong nuclear force overcomes electromagnetic repulsion. Hence, the existence of a force different from electromagnetic repulsion can be deduced from the experiments. Therefore, **B** is the correct answer.

38.C We know that

$$E_{max} = hf - \Phi$$

where E_{max} is the maximum kinetic energy of the emitted photoelectrons.

A graph of the variation of the maximum kinetic energy of photoelectrons with the frequency of the incident light has the equation $E_{max} = hf - \Phi$, where h is the gradient of the graph, f is the frequency and $-\Phi$ is the y-intercept. Since h (plank constant) has a constant value, it can be deduced that all graphs have the constant slope.

And so, the answer is option **C**.

39.B **[Memorize]** Half-life depends only on the type of substance decaying and doesn't depend on parameters such as mass, pressure, and temperature. Thus, doubling the mass has no effect on the half-life. Activity is defined as the number of nuclei decaying in a second. Thus, the more we have of the substance, higher the activity. Hence, doubling the mass of the substance will lead to a double in the activity.

And so, the answer is option **B**.

40.A We know that

$$Nuclear\ density = \frac{Mass\ of\ the\ nucleus}{Volume\ of\ the\ nucleus}$$

The protons and neutrons in the nucleus contribute to its mass and volume. As a consequence, addition of protons and neutrons to the nucleus (increase in nucleon number) will lead to an increase in both the mass and volume of the nucleus. Due to increase in both mass and volume, the ratio (nuclear density) will remain constant.

Therefore, the answer is option **A**.

November 2016

1.C To calculate momentum, we need to know the mass of the boy and his velocity when he lands. The boy stops moving once he reaches the ground, so the momentum change is simply the momentum he has while hitting the ground. We can calculate the velocity using the formula:

$$v^2 = u^2 + 2as$$

Where a is the acceleration which we can take to be 10 m/s^2 and so we know that

$$v^2 = 0 + 2(10)(3) = 60$$

and we can approximate v to be a value around 8 (more precisely something around 8.3). We can approximate the boy's mass to be $50kg$ and so the momentum will be $50 \times 8 = 400$ and this matches with 5×10^2 which is option **C,** and this is the correct answer.

2.C Speed does not depend on the direction of motion and since the object spends equal amount of time travelling at $3m/s$ and at $4m/s$ the average speed will be $3.5m/s$. Therefore, the correct answer is option **C.**

3.B We know that the integral of an acceleration-time graph is the velocity of the object (which is also the area under the graph) and so from this we know that the correct answer is option **B.**

Note: this question can also be solved by using units: a is m/s^2 and time is s so their product will give m/s which is the unit for velocity.

4.C Let us draw a free-body diagram to help us answer this question. By doing so, we can separate the tension into its vertical component and horizontal component.

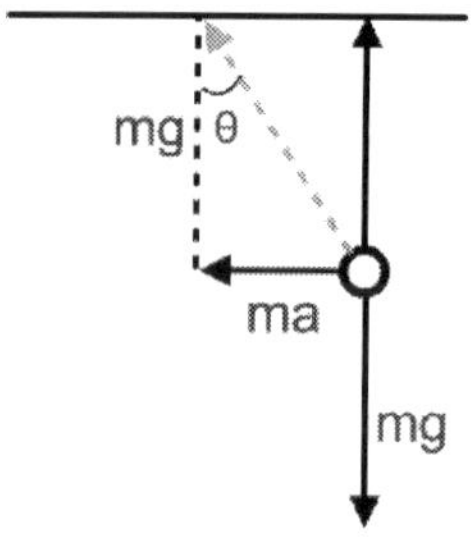

From this, we can see that the vertical component of tension is mg while the horizontal component of tension is ma and if we draw a right-angled triangle here:

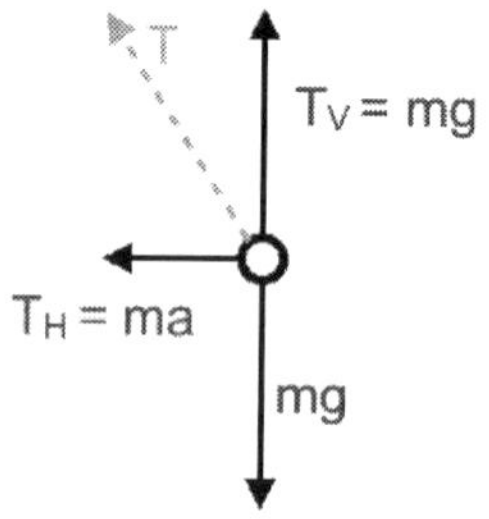

Then we know that $tan\theta = \frac{a}{g}$ and so $a = gtan\theta$ and therefore, the correct answer is option C.

5.A Since there is a constant force, we know that there is a constant acceleration (since $F = ma$) and so the velocity increases linearly (shown in options A and C). We also know that

$$kinetic\ energy = \frac{1}{2}mv^2$$

and so kinetic energy depends on the square of the velocity. If velocity increases linearly, then the kinetic energy will increase exponentially (like an x^2 graph) like the ones shown in options A and D. Therefore, the correct answer is option **A** which shows the correct graph for the kinetic energy as well as the velocity.

6.D Although B may seem the be the correct answer, it is not the case as the question is more complicated than it seems initially. The $2kg$ object is in regular free-fall and the acceleration is just g. But the situation is not that simple for the $1kg$ object. Before the thread is cut, the $1kg$ object has weight acting downwards and tension acting upwards.

The value of the weight is $3g$ and the tension is also $3g$ (this is because the combined mass of the 2 objects is $3kg$). But when the thread is cut, the weight acting downwards is only $1g$ as the $2kg$ object is no longer there, but the tension does not go away at the instant the thread is cut so the tension is still $3g$. Therefore, the net force is $2g$ and by using the formula $F = ma$ we can find out that the $a = 2g$ and so the correct answer is option **D**.

7.B We know that

$$kinetic\ energy = \frac{1}{2}mv^2$$

so, we need to find the value of v where the kinetic energy becomes 200J. So, we know that there is a change of 100J in the kinetic energy and this is the work done by gravity. We know that $W = Fscos\theta = mascos\theta$ and so we can substitute to get $100 = 2(10)(s)$ and so $s = \frac{100}{20} = 5$ which makes option **B** the correct answer.

8.D The change in potential energy of the student because he climbs 6m is given by: $600 \times 6 = 3600$. We can use the formula

$$Power = \frac{Energy}{time} = \frac{3600}{8} = 450W$$

to conclude that option **D** is the correct answer.

9.D Let us first deconstruct the graph. The first section where line slopes up is when it is a solid, the second section where the line slopes up is a liquid and the last section where the line slopes up is gaseous state. From the formula $Q = mc\Delta T$ we know that higher c would mean that you need more Q to achieve temperature change. If the gradient of the line is high, then that means that it takes less time for it to heat up and so it has a lower heat capacity. When the gradient is low, it takes much longer for it to heat up and so it has a higher heat capacity. The steepest slope is for liquid and so this means that it has lowest heat capacity, and the gentlest slope is for solid which means that it has the highest heat capacity. Therefore, the correct answer is option **D**.

10.B We know that pressure is caused by the molecules striking the walls of the containers. If the pressure decreases, then this is because the molecules are striking the walls less often which means that the correct answer is option **B**.

11.C The gradient of the graph is $\frac{V}{T}$ and we know that $pV = nRT$ and so $\frac{V}{T} = \frac{nR}{P}$

We know that $n = \frac{N}{N_A}$ and so $\frac{V}{T} = \frac{N\,R}{N_A P}$. From the equation $\frac{3}{2}K_B T = \frac{3\,R}{2N_A}T$ we can simplify to get

$$K_B = \frac{R}{N_A}$$

If we substitute that into the previous equation, we deduced that;

$$\frac{V}{T} = \frac{N\,R}{PN_A} = \frac{N}{P}K_B = \frac{NK_B}{P}$$

which is option **C.**

12.D We know that the minimum kinetic energy is reached at two distinct times in one oscillation. These two points are at the two ends of the oscillation which means that they happen when the object has travelled $\frac{1}{4}$ of the oscillation and $\frac{3}{4}$ of the oscillation. This is reflected in the graph in option **D** and so this is the correct answer.

Note: the movement starts from the center and reaches maximum displacement on the right and then passes through the center and reaches the maximum displacement on the left and finishes one oscillation when it passes the center again.

13.A Since the refractive index of diamond is more than 1, it means that the diamond is more optically dense than air. Therefore, we know that light travels faster in diamond than in air. We know the formula

$$\frac{sin\theta_2}{sin\theta_1} = \frac{v2}{v1}$$

and so, this means that the angle formed in air is more than the angle in diamond. But if we look at options B, C and D, we can see that the angle in air is less or equal to angle in diamond which is incorrect. Therefore, the only remaining option is **A** and that is the correct answer.

Note: total internal reflection can happen only when light goes from optically denser medium to optically rarer medium (just like the one shown in option A). Moreover, the angle in air for option A can be taken to be the obtuse angle from the normal line to the reflected line and thus this reaffirms the fact that the angle in air is higher than the angle in diamond.

14.B Recall from section 4.3 of the data booklet that:

$$I \propto A^2$$

Also recall that as distance from source increases, light intensity drops at a squared rate (i.e., $I \propto x^{-2}$). We can combine these expressions and add a constant k to go from a proportional-to statement to an equation for the original intensity:

$$I = \frac{kA_0^{\ 2}}{x^2}$$

Now we have an equation, we can substitute our new values for I and x to work out how A changes:

$$2I = \frac{kA^2}{(2x)^2}$$

Given that k hasn't changed, we must maintain equality to the original expression. Right now, the left side of the equation is twice as big ($2I$ vs I) but the right side is 4 times smaller. To mitigate this, A^2 must become 8 times larger than $(A_0)^2$.

Therefore, A must become $\sqrt{8} = 2\sqrt{2}$ times bigger than A_0. This option is found in **B**.

15.A There are two key points to note here. The first one is that the wavefront bends towards the object (which is shown in options A and C). The second point is that there is an empty region that forms behind the object due to the diffraction (as shown in options A and B). Therefore, the correct answer is option **A**.

16. C Because the relative influence on the electric field of each charge reduces as distance increases, and the $+10\mu C$ charge is double the magnitude of the $-5\mu C$ charge, we need to find a point which is further from the positive charge than the negative one, which is option **C.**

---

17. C Iterating through each statement:

A. The additional resistor can be considered to be attached in series, so total resistance is 4Ω. As current is $voltage/resistance$, I is 3A, so A is **incorrect**

B. The 'load' can be considered the external resistor <u>only</u>, and as this external resistor only represents half of total resistance, the p.d across it is only 6V, so B is **incorrect**

C. $P = VI$. As per statement A, the current in this series circuit (which is constant throughout it) is 3A, and as per our work on statement B, the voltage within the battery is 6V. Therefore, power dissipated is 18W and C is **correct**

D. As per our work in A, resistance in the circuit is 4Ω, so D is **incorrect**

Therefore, the correct answer is option **C.**

Note: In fact, total resistance is 4 regardless of whether the resistor is in series or parallel, in this case.

18.B As per section 5.4 of the data booklet:

$$F = BIL\ sin\theta$$

Let's substitute our new values in to see how F changes:

$$F_2 = (2B)\left(\frac{I}{4}\right)Lsin\theta = \left(\frac{2}{4}\right)BILsin\theta = \frac{1}{2}F$$

This corresponds to **B.**

19. A

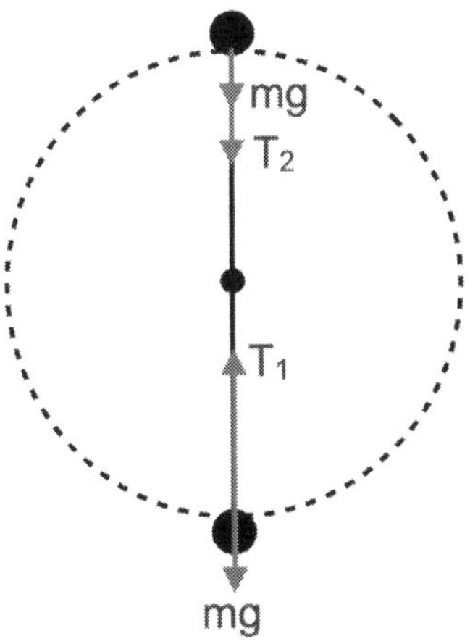

Remember that the net force (in this case, the sum of tension and gravitational force) is always equal to the centripetal force,

$$T_1 + mg = \frac{mv^2}{r}$$

At the highest point, tension, and gravity act in the same direction, so the above equation applies:

$$T_1 = \frac{mv^2}{r} - mg$$

However, at the lowest point, mg acts downward while tension acts upwards towards the center, so

$$T_2 = \frac{mv^2}{r} + mg$$

These represent the two extremes of direction for tension and gravity. We can therefore say that tension is highest at the lowest point, option **A**

---

20. A **[Memorize]** For alpha (α), beta (β) and gamma (γ) particles:

For penetrating ability:

$\alpha < \beta < \gamma$

For ionizing power:

$\gamma < \beta < \alpha$

Therefore, the correct answer is option **A.**

---

21. B An alpha particle adds 4 to the mass number (14 for N) and 2 to the atomic number (7 for N). As a proton is also produced, we remove one from the mass number and one from the atomic number. The result has a mass number of 17 and atomic number of 8, which corresponds to **B.**

22. C The mass defect is equivalent to binding energy. We simply need to convert mass to energy using

$$E = mc^2$$

We can use the value for the speed of light and apply this equation to get energy in Joules, and then convert to eV.

$$E_{Joules} = (4 \times 10^{-30})(3 \times 10^{8})^2 = 3.6 \times 10^{-13}$$

To convert from Joules to eV, divide by the unified atomic mass unit and then multiply by 10^6 to go from MeV to eV:

$$E = \frac{3.6 \times 10^{-13}}{1.661 \times 10^{-27}} \times 10^6 \approx 2.167 \times 10^{14}$$

Using one significant figure on this yields option **C.**

---

23. A **[Memorize]** A photovoltaic cell converts solar to electrical energy, while a solar heating panel converts solar to thermal energy. Therefore, option **A** is the correct answer.

---

24. B **[Memorize]** The solar constant is defined as the intensity of the Sun's radiation at the mean distance from the Sun of the Earth's orbit around the Sun. Therefore, **B** is correct.

---

25. A The equation for the relationship between emitted power, temperature, and surface area is found in section 8.2:

$$P = e\sigma AT^4$$

For black-body Y, as its temperature is <u>double</u> that of X, its T^4 term is $2^4 = 16$ times greater than X. As a result, the surface area of X should be 16 times that of Y. Because area is proportional to radius squared, we must square-root this to find the ratio of radii, which is 4. This corresponds to option **A.**

26. C As per section 9.1 of the data booklet, the total energy of an SHM system is:

$$E_T = \frac{1}{2}m\omega^2 x_0^2$$

We also know two more things: 1) E_T is constant as long as x_0, the maximum displacement, doesn't change (which it doesn't) and 2) $E_T = E_K + E_P$. We have the equation for kinetic energy:

$$E_k = \frac{1}{2}m\omega^2\left(x_0^2 - x^2\right)$$

Because of point 2), we know therefore that the equation for potential energy is:

$$E_P = \frac{1}{2}m\omega^2\left(x^2\right)$$

The question states that the particle is 0.20x_0 <u>away</u> from maximum displacement, which means that x, current displacement, is actually equal to $0.80x_0$.
Substituting that into the equation for E_P yields the following:

$$E_p = \frac{1}{2}m\omega^2(0.8x_0)^2 = \frac{1}{2}m\omega^2\left(0.64x_0^2\right) = 0.64E_T$$

This corresponds to option **C.**

---

27. D **[Memorize]** The interference pattern for light incident on a double slit is a <u>sequence</u> of maxima, each made up of smaller, equal-width subsidiary maxima (as seen in option **D)**

---

28. C Let's split the observed light into two halves – left and right. Each half represents an angular width of 90° (as the maximum coverage of a diffraction grating is 180°). The number of maxima observed for each half can be calculated using the formula:

$$n = \frac{d\sin\theta}{\lambda}$$

Substituting our values for θ and d yields the following:

$$n = \frac{1}{\lambda} \times \frac{7\lambda}{2} = \frac{7}{2}$$

The reason why n for a given side is not a whole number is because each includes half of the central maxima. Multiplying by two to combine the left and right sides yields answer **C.**

29. B This is a question on resolution. We use the expression from section 9.4 of the data booklet to determine the conditions needed for resolution:

$$\frac{\lambda}{\Delta\lambda} = mN$$

The question asked for wavelength difference, so let's isolate $\Delta\lambda$ and substitute our known values:

$$\Delta\lambda = \frac{\lambda}{mN} = \frac{400 \times 10^{-9}}{100 \times 2} = 2 \times 10^{-9}$$

This corresponds to option **B.**

---

30. B Let's recall the equation involving G rearrange to make G the subject:

$$F = \frac{GMm}{r^2} \quad \text{so} \quad G = \frac{Fr^2}{Mm}$$

Let's now replace each term of the equation with its unit:

$$\frac{(N)(m^2)}{(kg)(kg)} = Nm^2kg^{-2}$$

Let's now combine it with the units of ϵ_0, which are stated in the constants section of the data booklet:

$$Nm^2kg^{-2} \times C^2N^{-1}m^{-2} = N^{1-1}m^{2-2}kg^{-2}C^2 = C^2kg^{-2}$$

This corresponds to option **B.**

---

31. B

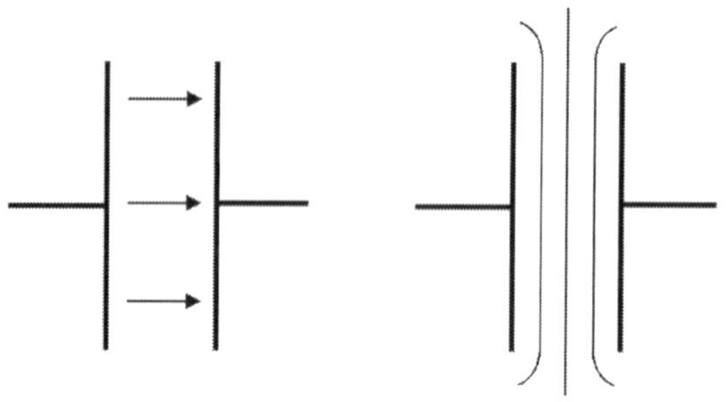

[Memorize] Equipotential field lines are always <u>perpendicular</u> to field lines

This means we need straight, vertical lines through the midsection between the plates, which curve at the top and bottom so that they're always tangential to the arcs. Specifically, **B** is the correct answer.

32. A Recall that, as a mass gets closer to the Earth, its gravitational potential becomes more negative. Therefore, because the satellite's potential actually gets larger, we know the satellite is moving away from Earth, narrowing our choices to A and B. Let's calculate the change in GPE. Gravitational potential is GPE per unit mass. Therefore, to calculate change in GPE, we calculate the change in gravitational potential and multiply by mass, which equals $10 \times 1500\text{MJ} = 15\text{GJ}$. This corresponds to option **A.**

---

33. D Iterating through the four options:

A. Using thinner wires will increase resistance as it provides less avenues for current to flow. This reduce efficiency, a **Negative effect.**

B. A solid core would increase energy losses by increasing the incidence of eddy currents. **Negative effect**

C. Soft magnetic material is the most effective as the transformer core. Iron is a soft magnetic material. Steel isn't, so incorporating it has a **negative effect**

D. By process of elimination, we could conclude that the answer is **D.** 'Linking more flux' is another way of saying increasing total flux. Ensuring higher flux linkage maximizes the rate of change of flux linkage, increasing efficiency.

Therefore, the correct answer is **D.**

34.A We know that the current flowing is alternating current and so we need to analyze how the current flows in two situations. First let us analyze what happens when the current moves clockwise. The diode at the top will allow the current to pass through while the bottom diode will not allow current to pass through and this means that current approaches X from the left.

When the current moves in the anticlockwise direction, the bottom diode will allow the current to pass through while the top diode will not allow the current to pass through and this means that the current approaches X from the left once again.
From this, we know two main things about the potential difference. The first one is that since the current is continuous, the potential difference is continuous. The second point is that since the current is always in the same direction, there should be no change in the sign of the potential difference graph. Therefore, the only graph that fits the above conditions is the graph in option **A.**

35.C We can apply the formula

$$E = \frac{1}{2}CV^2$$

and we know that $C = \varepsilon\frac{A}{d}$. When a sheet of dielectric is placed in between the plates of the capacitor, the permittivity (ε) increases as the permittivity of the sheet is higher than the permittivity of air. So, since we know that permittivity increases, this results in an increase in the capacitance which in turn leads to an increase in the energy. Therefore, the correct answer is option **C**.

36.A The formula for calculating capacitance of two capacitors connected in parallel is

$$C_T = C_1 + C_2$$

And so, this means that the total capacitance of the two connected in parallel is

$$C_T = 1 + 1 = 2$$

The formula for calculating capacitors of two capacitors connected in series is

$$\frac{1}{C_T} = \frac{1}{C_1} + \frac{1}{C_2}$$

And so, this means that the total capacitance of the two connected in series is

$$\frac{1}{C_T} = \frac{1}{2} + \frac{1}{2} = 1$$

Therefore, the total capacitance of the circuit is $\frac{1}{1} = 1$ which is option **A**.

37.D We must note that energy and momentum are both conserved in all particle interactions in the physical world. Consequently, both energy and momentum are conserved in the pair production process. Therefore, the answer is **D**.

38.D Let's work with units. It is fairly obvious that the correct solution should have the same unit as that of speed (ms^{-1}) since it is the uncertainty in the speed of the electron. Let's find the individual units of h, r and m and then use those units to compute the units of each of the options. The option with the unit ms^{-1} is the correct solution.

Unit of m (mass) : kg (obvious!)

Unit of r (position) : m

Unit of h (plank constant) : Js (in data booklet!)

Since Joules is not an SI unit, we can simplify the unit of h even more. We know that kinetic energy (in Joules) = $\frac{1}{2}mv^2$. Thus Joules = $kg\,m^2s^{-2}$

Now let's use substitution to find the unit of plank constant in terms of SI base units

Unit of h (plank constant) : $kg\,m^2s^{-2}s = kg\,m^2s^{-1}$ (J was substituted with $kg\,m^2s^{-2}$)

Now let's use the above units to calculate the final units of each option.

Option A:

$$\frac{kg\,m^2s^{-1}}{m} = kg\,ms^{-1}$$

Option B:

$$\frac{kg\,m^3s^{-1}}{kg} = m^3s^{-1}$$

Option C:

$$\frac{kg^2\,m^2s^{-1}}{m} = kg^2\,ms^{-1}$$

Option D:

$$\frac{kg\,m^2s^{-1}}{m \cdot kg} = ms^{-1}$$

Hence, it is clear that only option D has the unit ms^{-1}, which corresponds with that of speed. Therefore, the answer is **D**.

39.B We know that emitted beta particles have a continuous kinetic energy spectrum and therefore don't provide evidence for the existence of discrete nuclear energy levels. On the contrary, energy emissions from the decay of alpha particles are discrete. Similarly, Gamma rays are emitted in discrete energies corresponding to the energy state transitions a nuclide may undergo when in an excited state. Therefore, the spectrum of alpha particle energies and gamma ray energies provide evidence for the existence of nuclear energy levels. And so the correct answer is option **B**.

40.D The word electron in electron antineutrino might be deceiving and may lead you to think that the charge is negative. But note the word neutrino, which means neutral charge or zero charge.

[Memorise] The electron neutrino (ν) is a subatomic lepton elementary particle which has zero net electric charge. Its anti-particle also has zero charge.

Also note that in a beta minus decay, a neutron is converted to a proton and the process creates an electron and an electron antineutrino. In a positive beta decay (β+ decay), a proton in the parent nucleus decays into a neutron that remains in the daughter nucleus, and the nucleus emits a neutrino and a positron. These facts are directly mentioned in the textbook and you must know them prior to the examination. Therefore, the answer is **D**.

1.C We know that

$$Energy = work = F \times s = m \times a \times s = m \times \frac{\Delta v}{t} \times s$$

Unit of $m = kg$

Unit of $\Delta v = ms^{-1}$

Unit of $t = s$

Unit of $s = m$

Hence, unit of Energy = $kg \times \frac{m}{s} \times \frac{1}{s} \times m = kgm^2s^{-2}$

Therefore, the answer is **C.**

2.B The gradient of distance-time graph represents velocity, and the gradient of velocity-time graph represents acceleration. In the given velocity-time graph, velocity increases from 0 to maximum and then decreases back to 0. This shows that the object initially accelerates (since there is an increase in velocity over time) and then decelerates (since there is a decrease in velocity over time). When we look at option B, it is clear that the gradient of the distance-time graph (which represents velocity) increases (as the steepness of the curve increases) after which it decreases (since the steepness of the graph decreases). This corresponds with increase in velocity over time (acceleration) followed by decrease in velocity over time (deceleration) in the original velocity-time graph. Therefore, the answer is **B.**

3.C Area under the acceleration-time graph represents change in speed

$$\frac{m}{s^2} \times s = ms^{-1}$$

Thus, the change in speed (below) corresponds to **C**:

$$= \frac{1}{2} \times 12 \times 6 = 36\ ms^{-1}$$

4.B We know that resultant force = ma.

Weight acts downwards and tension force (in the elevator cable) acts upwards.

Thus, resultant force, $ma = mg - T$

$$T = mg - ma = m(g - a)$$

$$= 750 * (10 - 2)$$

$$= 6000\ N$$

$$= 6.0\ kN$$

Therefore, the answer is **B.**

5.A A useful equation to know is

$v = A(amplitude) \times \omega\ (angular\ velocity)$

where $A = y$

We also know that

$$\omega = \frac{2\pi}{T}$$

Moreover, we can find T using

$$T = 2\pi\sqrt{\frac{m}{k}}$$

From the second and third equation we can deduce that

$$\frac{2\pi}{\omega} = 2\pi\sqrt{\frac{m}{k}}$$

$$\omega = \sqrt{\frac{k}{m}}$$

From the first and third equation we can deduce that

$$v = y \times \sqrt{\frac{k}{m}}$$

Therefore, the answer is **A.**

6.D We know that

$$P = Fv$$

We also know that

$$v = \frac{distance}{time}$$

Combining the first and second equation gives

$$P\ (power) = F \times \frac{distance}{time}$$

$$= 1500 \times \frac{100}{5}$$

$$= 30\ kW$$

Therefore, the answer is **D.**

7.B We know that

$$F = \frac{\Delta p}{\Delta t}$$

At the specific instant,

$$\frac{\Delta p}{\Delta t} = resultant\ force = 40 - 10 = 30\ kgms^{-2}$$

Therefore, the answer is **B.**

8.A During freezing, the temperature is constant. This is because during the phase change from liquid to solid, the extra energy extracted is used to convert the liquid to solid rather than reduce the temperature. Heat is stored in the form of potential energy which is used in bond formation (conversion of liquid to solid). Therefore, the answer is **A.**

9.A We know that

$$Pressure = \frac{Force}{Area}$$

where the force is equal to the weight of the cylinder.

We also know that area of the cylinder wall on the flat surface is

$\pi \times R^2\ (area\ of\ the\ outer\ circle) - \pi \times (R - x)^2\ (area\ of\ the\ inner\ circle) = 2\pi Rx + x^2$

Since R is much greater than x (mentioned in the question), it can be assumed that x is negligible and thus equal to 0.

Hence, combining the first and second equation gives

$$Pressure = \frac{W}{2\pi Rx}$$

Therefore, the answer is **A.**

10.C We know that

$$PV = nRT$$

And so,

$$V = \frac{nRT}{P}$$

We also know that

$$\bar{E}_k(kinetic\ energy) = \frac{3}{2}k_B T$$

Since the mean kinetic energy of the particles in the gas doubles, it is apparent that the temperature also doubles ($\frac{3}{2}k_B$ is a constant).

As the temperature doubles and pressure remains constant (given in the question), the volume of the gas doubles (look at the first equation). nR is constant since R is a constant and number of moles of a fixed mass of ideal gas remains the same.
Therefore, the answer is **C.**

11.A Remember that the first derivative of velocity gives the acceleration. So, you differentiate the velocity to get acceleration. The given velocity-time graph in the question has the equation $y = -cos(t)$ (you'll know this if you are a Math HL student!). The equation of acceleration-time graph can be found by finding the derivative of $-cos(t)$, which is $sin(t)$. Hence, the equation of the acceleration-time graph is $y = -sin(t)$. Option A is the only option that corresponds with this equation (it is a positive sine graph). Therefore, the answer is **A.**

Alternative solution (for those of you who are not in Math HL!)
Gradient of the velocity-time graph gives the acceleration. The gradient of the velocity-time graph at time 0 is 0 (thus, the acceleration-time graph starts at the origin) after which it is positive and increases (as the slope of the curve increases). This trend corresponds with only option A. Therefore, the answer is **A.**

12.B The time period of this wave is 5.0ms while its speed is 40m/s. From the wave's time period we can find out its frequency using

$$f = \frac{1}{T}$$

Therefore, we get a frequency of 200Hz. Then by using

$$c = f\lambda$$

And so, the wavelength of this wave will be

$$\lambda = 40/200$$

Since the wavelength is 0.2m, we know that the phase difference between two points at a distance of 0.2m is 2π. Now, for a distance of 0.05m the corresponding phase difference would be $\pi/2$ since 0.05 is 1/4th of 0.2m. Therefore, the answer is **B.**

13.C **[Remember]** Polarization is only possible with transverse waves. The reason for this is that the vibrations of the transverse waves occur in all directions perpendicular to the direction of travel, so it is possible to confine these vibrations to a single wave. Vibrations of the longitudinal waves occur only in the same direction as the direction of travel, hence, cannot be polarized. Sound waves are longitudinal waves, so cannot be polarized. Therefore, the answer is **C.**

14.C We know that

$$I = \frac{I_0}{2}\cos^2\theta$$

where $\frac{I_0}{2}$ is the intensity of the polarized wave after passing through the first polarizing sheet

The question tells us that the intensity of light emerging from the second sheet is $\frac{I_0}{4}$

Hence,

$$I = \frac{I_0}{4}$$

Substituting I as $\frac{I_0}{4}$ in the first equation gives

$$\frac{I_0}{4} = \frac{I_0}{2}\cos^2\theta$$

$$\theta = \cos^{-1}\frac{1}{2}$$

Therefore, the correct answer is option **C.**

15.D For a pipe closed on only one end, the distance between two nodes is always

$$\frac{\lambda}{2}$$

where λ is the wavelength of the wave. From the diagram we know that this distance is x and therefore, the wavelength can be found out by equation

$$x = \frac{\lambda}{2}$$

And so $\lambda = 2x$. Therefore, the correct answer is option **D**.

16.C The change in kinetic energy can be found by using the formula

$$W = qV$$

The charge of an electron q can be taken from the data booklet and we know that the value of V is 2.5MV. By substituting the values, we get the change in energy to be 0.4pJ (for conversion from Joules to picoJoules, please refer to data booklet). Therefore, the correct answer is option **C**.

17.D Current is simply the charge passing through one second, this is simply

$$nAvq$$

where N is number of electrons, A is area of cylinder, v is the velocity of electrons and q is the charge of electrons. The length of the cylinder is simply the velocity of the electrons (in one second as this is how long we are interested in calculating charge) and so we have

$$Av = V$$

where V is the volume of the cylinder. Multiplying the volume by the number of electrons per cubic meter, n, gives us the total amount of electrons N. From here we know that

$$I = Nq$$

$$I = Ne \text{ (since } q = e\text{)}$$

$$N = \frac{I}{e}$$

Therefore, the correct answer is option **D**.

18.A Since the particle is travelling parallel to the magnetic field (i.e., it does not cut the magnetic field therefore never causing a change to the magnetic flux) there will be no force acting on an alpha particle, thus giving us option **A**. Remember that there will only be a force when the angle between the alpha particle and the magnetic field is not 0.

19.A We know that the formula for centripetal force is

$$F = \frac{mv^2}{r}$$

If you substitute all the values given in the table into the above equation (changing the respective v and r values, you will see that option **A** gives you the same amount of centripetal force that you would get with an object of mass m, velocity v and radius r.

20.D After a time of 4T has passed, Nuclide A has gone through 4 half-lives and Nuclide B has gone through 2 half-lives. Therefore, for Nuclide A the activity would be 1/16 of what it was initially and for B it would be ¼ of what it was initially. Remember that at each half life, the nuclide loses half its activity. Therefore, the ratio of the activity of Nuclide A to Nuclide B would be ¼ which is option **D.**

21.A **[Memorize]** An atomic mass unit is 1/12th of the mass of a neutral Carbon-12 atom. Therefore, the correct answer is option **A.**

22.A In nuclear fission, a bigger atom is broken into two smaller atoms while releasing a huge amount of energy. Therefore, for a very big atom the binding energy per nucleon will be smaller than the corresponding value for a very small atom (after Iron). Since there is a huge amount of energy released in this process, we know that the binding energy of Y and Z will be more than the binding energy of X, leading us to option **A.**

23.B The process of convection cannot happen in the moon as there is no atmosphere and thus no air. However, conduction and radiation are possible on the surface of the moon as conduction happens through the ground (solid) and radiation takes place in the vacuum above the surface of the moon. This gives us option **B** as the right answer.

24.D We know that

$$b = \lambda_{max} T$$

and so, if the temperature of planet X is less, then it needs to have a higher λ_{max}. Since the intensity is dependent on temperature a lower temperature would mean that the planet has a lower intensity than planet Y at that point. This gives us option **D** to be the right answer.

25.D The formula for calculating albedo is

$$albedo = \frac{total\ scattered\ power}{total\ incident\ power}$$

so, the power scattered will be 0.25 while the total incident power would be 1. So, when calculating the ratio asked in the question

$$\frac{power\ absorbed\ by\ glacier\ ice}{power\ incident\ on\ glacier\ ice}$$

we replace the respective values and get

$$\frac{0.75}{0.25} = 3$$

Keep in mind that the power absorbed is the difference between the total power and the amount of power scattered. And so, the correct answer is option **D.**

26.C The time period of an oscillation is given by the formula

$$T = 2\pi\sqrt{\frac{l}{g}}$$

For mercury this would be

$$T_{mercury} = 2\pi\sqrt{\frac{l}{0.4g}}$$

Which is the same as

$$T_{mercury} = 2\pi\sqrt{\frac{l}{g}}\cdot\sqrt{\frac{1}{0.4}}$$

$\sqrt{\frac{1}{0.4}} = 1.6$. Therefore, the time period is approximately 1.6 times the time period when the satellite is orbiting around earth. Thus, option **C** is the correct answer.

27.B **[Memorize]** We need coherent waves for double-slit interference and their properties state that these waves must be of the same frequency and must have 0 or constant phase difference. This leads us to option **B.**

28.A This question is about Doppler effect. From the data booklet, we know that the formula for moving source is

$$f' = f\left(\frac{v}{v \pm u_s}\right)$$

And for moving observer is

$$f' = f\left(\frac{v \pm u_o}{v}\right)$$

For the moving source scenario, since the source is moving towards the cliff we have

$$f' = f\left(\frac{c}{c - u}\right)$$

And for a moving observer, since the observer is moving towards the cliff again we have

$$f' = f\left(\frac{c + u}{c}\right)$$

Remember that in both these scenarios we can decide whether to use + or – by figuring out whether the receiving frequency will be more or less than the initial frequency. In essence, when source and observer are relatively moving closer to each other, the receiving frequency is always higher than the emitting frequency.

The final frequency for the moving source scenario becomes the initial frequency for the moving observer scenario and so this becomes

$$f\left(\frac{c}{c - u}\right) \cdot \left(\frac{c + u}{c}\right)$$

Which is simply

$$\frac{c + u}{c - u}$$

This gives us option **A.**

29.B From the data booklet, we know that

$$E = -\frac{\Delta V_e}{\Delta r}$$

where V_e is the electric potential and r is the separation distance between the plates Between the two plates, we have uniform electric field, so electric field strength is constant.

If we rearrange the above formula, we get

$$\Delta V_e = -E\Delta r$$

From the rearranged formula, it is clear that electric potential is proportional to distance. Therefore, the answer is **B.**

30.C We know that

$$W = F_g = \frac{Gm_1m_2}{r^2}$$

As the radius is doubled, r^2 increases by a factor of 4. Therefore, W decreases by a factor of 4. In other words, W becomes $0.25W$.
Similarly, we know that

$$E_p = \frac{-GMm}{r}$$

As r is doubled, E_p decreases by a factor of 2 (since r increases by a factor of 2).
Therefore, E_p becomes $\frac{E_p}{2} = 0.5E_p$.
Hence, the answer is **C**.

31.B Electric field strength is the force the field would induce on a unit electric charge. Let's choose to place a positively charged particle in each possible location:

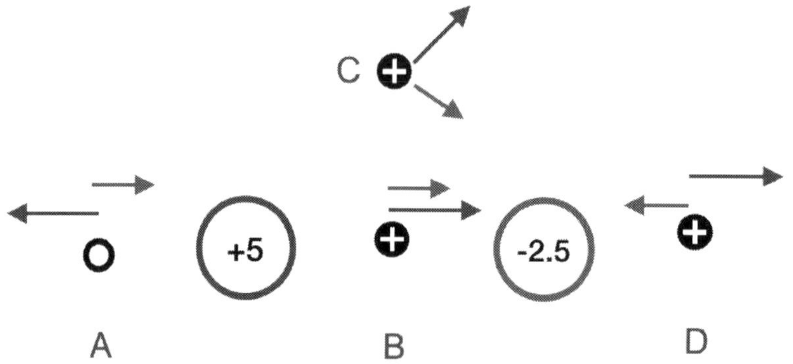

A. Here, the particle will be repelled (going left) by the $5\mu C$ charge but attracted (going right) to the $-2.5\mu C$ charge so the net force is reduced.
B. Here, the particle will be repelled (going right) by the positive charge but also attracted to the right by the negative one, so the magnitude of force is higher than A
C. From the diagram, you can see the horizontal components of the forces are added together but the vertical component of each force acts in opposite directions, so net force is lower than in B
D. Here, the particle is repelled rightwards but attracted leftwards, so net force is lower than B

Clearly, the force is highest at **B**.

32.D For alternating electric current, root mean square (rms) is the value of the direct current that would produce the same average power dissipation.
Thus,

$$I_{rms} = 5A$$

From section 11.2 of the data booklet, we know that

$$I_0 = I_{rms} \times \sqrt{2}$$

where I_0 is the peak value of alternating current

$$I_0 = 5 \times \sqrt{2}\ A$$

Therefore, the answer is **D**.

33.B **[Memorize]** The unit of magnetic flux is Weber (Wb), and the unit of magnetic field strength is Tesla (T). This makes option **B** the correct answer.

34.C Some energy is dissipated as heat in the resistor, which leads to energy loss. Consequently, the energy stored in the capacitor is the difference between the total energy supplied by the battery and energy lost due to the resistor. Hence, $E_b > E_c$. Therefore, the answer is **C**.

35.B We know the relationship between charge and current,

$$I = \frac{\Delta q}{\Delta t}$$

$$\Delta q = I \times \Delta t$$

where q is the charge, I is the current and t is time.
Now let's substitute actual values given in the question to calculate charge,

$$\Delta q = 2.5 \times 10^{-6} \times 100 = 250\ \mu C$$

Next let's look for the formula of capacitance in the data booklet,

$$C = \frac{Q}{V}$$

where C is capacitance, Q is charge and V is the potential difference.
Now all we need to do is substitute values of charge and potential difference to calculate the capacitance of the capacitor

$$C = \frac{250\ \mu C}{5.0\ V} = 50\ \mu F$$

Therefore, the answer is **B**.

36.D This question is a simple application of Fleming's left-hand rule. Let's first test option D. Remember to use your left hand. Your index finger should point in the direction of the magnetic field (into the page). Your middle finger should point in the direction of the current (in this case left side since we are testing the side of the coil that contains option D). You will notice that your thumb points downwards which indicates that option D is correct. Therefore, the answer is **D.**

37.A The average radius of a nucleus with A nucleons is

$$R = R_0 A^{\frac{1}{3}}$$

where $R_0 = 1.2 \times 10^{-15}$. Since R_0 is the same for all nucleus, the radius (and thus diameter) only depends on the value of A. So, the radius for silver would be:

$$R = R_0(108)^{\frac{1}{3}} = R_0(4.5)$$

Now we need a nucleus which has a radius that is approximately

$$R_0\left(\frac{4.5}{3}\right) = R_0(1.5)$$

This means that we need $A^{\frac{1}{3}} = 1.5$ and thus $A = 1.5^3 = 3.4 \approx 4$. Therefore, the nucleus of the atom we need has 4 nucleons and thus the correct answer is Helium which is option **A.**

Note: in this question, we worked with radius instead of diameter as diameter is just a constant multiple of radius and so multiplying both quantities by 2 would not make any change to their ratio. Simply put, if X has a radius of 2 and Y has a radius of 6, then the diameter of X is 4 and the diameter of Y is 12 and thus both quantities of Y are three times the respective quantities of X.

38.D From section 12.1 of the data booklet, we know that

$$P(r) = \Delta V \times |\psi|^2$$

where $P(r)$ is the probability that an electron will be found within a small volume ΔV and ψ is the wave function

Notice that the square of the wave function is used in the calculation of the probability of finding an electron in a particular region of space.

Therefore, the answer is **D.**

39.D We know that,

$$E = hf = \frac{hc}{\lambda} \left(since\ f = \frac{c}{\lambda} \right)$$

where E is the energy of the photon, λ is the wavelength, c is the speed of light and h is plank's constant. Since the electron moves away, we know it gains kinetic energy. This kinetic energy is gained from the photon and thus the energy of the photon decreases.

Since energy is inversely proportional to wavelength (which also means that wavelength is inversely proportional to frequency), when energy decreases, it results in an increase in wavelength. Therefore, the correct answer is option **D.**

40.D **[Memorize]** When proton absorbs an electron, a neutron and electron neutrino is produced. So, the correct answer is option **D.**

1. D When a variable with uncertainty is squared, its percentage uncertainty is doubled, so the percentage uncertainty in d is:

$$\frac{0.2}{2.0} \times 2 = 0.2 = 20\%$$

Multiplying this by the depth, d, gives the absolute uncertainty:

$$0.2 \times 20 = 4\text{m}$$

Therefore, the correct answer is option **D.**

---

2. B Remember that vertical and horizontal acceleration of the projectile are independent of each other. Because there is no other vertical force than gravity (as the projectile is initially fired horizontally), we do not actually need the value of 2km. Instead, we simply need the SUVAT relation:

$$s = ut - \frac{1}{2}at^2$$

Because it is fired horizontally, initial vertical velocity, u, is 0. Given that all answers are multiples of 10, we shall take g to be 10ms^{-2}:

$$s = 0 - \frac{1}{2} \times 10 \times 4^2 = 80m$$

Therefore, the correct answer is option **B.**

3. D Let's decode the information given into measurable statements:

1. The strings are of an equal length

   This implies that each string's angle relative to horizontal is the same, so they each experience the same magnitude of force

2. The strings are almost horizontal

   This implies that θ in the diagram below is small - below 45° and therefore that the vertical component of T is smaller than its horizontal component.

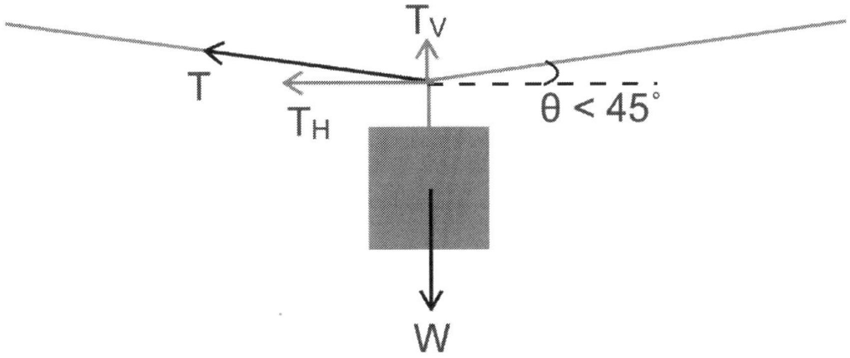

Remember that the combined vertical components of tension in each string need to oppose the vertical force of weight. Because vertical tension T_V is such a small proportion of T (less than half of it), even when using the combined tension from both strings, overall tension T needs to be higher than W to ensure $2T_V = W$. Hence, the answer is **D**.

4. C There isn't an immediate link between the forces specified and acceleration on the trolley. The force needed is actually the friction experienced between the block and the trolley. The formula for friction given the coefficient of dynamic friction is:

$$F_f = \mu_f \times N$$

Where N is the normal reaction force, equal to the weight of the block in newtons ($1.0\text{kg} \times 10$). Given the friction force of 3N, we use the mass of the trolley to work out it's acceleration:

$$a = \frac{F}{m} = \frac{3}{4.0} = 0.75\text{ms}^{-2}$$

So, option **C** is the correct answer.

---

5. B The question mentions kinetic energy, so the best approach is to use energy functions, specifically that between kinetic and gravitational potential energy at Earth's surface:

$$mgh = \frac{1}{2}mv^2$$

While height is proportional to the square of velocity, this isn't relevant to the question. The important thing is that height, *h*, is proportional to KE:

$$m \times gh = KE$$

After two bounces, KE has halved twice, so is at $^1/_4$ of its original height. Consequently, height has fallen by the same proportion, answer **B**.

---

6. D This is a question about momentum. We need a formula that equates mass, velocity, time, and force:

$$Ft = m\Delta v$$

The ball is initially at $4ms^{-1}$ and then becomes still when it sticks to the sensor. In this equation F also refers to average force, which is half of F_{max}. Let's substitute that in (note that 40ms is 0.04s):

$$\frac{F_{max}}{2} \times (0.04) = 0.2 \times (4.0 - 0.0)$$

Evaluating this equation gives a value of F_{max} as 40N, answer **D**.

7. D The initial momentum of 0 is conserved. As momentum is mass × velocity, and the ratio of mass number of lead-206 to an alpha particle is $^{206}/_{4}$, the relative velocity is correspondingly $\frac{4}{206}$, and so the correct answer is option **D**.

---

8. C The transition of ice at 5 °C to water at 50 °C has three distinct steps:

1. Ice gains 5 °C to become ice at melting point

$$E_1 = (\Delta T) \times m \times (c) = 5mc_i$$

2. Ice at 0 °C becomes water at the same temperature

$$E_2 = mL$$

3. Water at 0 °C gains 50 °C

$$E_3 = 50mc_w$$

Summing all energy changes gives the expression of answer **C**.

9.A The formula for energy is

$$E_K = \frac{3}{2}K_B T$$

and we know that K_B is a constant so the kinetic energy depends on the temperature of the container. Since the temperature of the container is constant for both the oxygen and nitrogen (because they are in the same container), the average kinetic energy is the same for both which leads to the ratio being 1 and so option **A** is the correct answer.

10.B From the formula

$$pV = nRT$$

we can rewrite it to get $p - \frac{nRT}{V}$. The initial temperature is 20℃ which means 293K and the final temperature is 40℃ which is 313K. Now, if we substitute the value we have into the equation for p, we get:

$$100 = nR \cdot \frac{293}{15}$$

and so, the value of $nR = 1500/293$. Now if we use this value obtained to find the pressure when the volume is changed we have:

$$p = \frac{nRT}{V} = \frac{\left(\frac{1500}{293}\right) \cdot 313}{5} = 320.47 \approx 320kPA$$

and this gives option **B** to be the correct answer.

11.D The formula for SHM is $a = -kx$ where a is the acceleration while x is the displacement and so the answer is option **D**.

12.B Let us notice the motion of particles at the juncture where $x = 1$ and $x = 3$. At $x = 3$, when x > 3 the particles are moving towards the right and when x < 3 the particles are moving to the left (essentially like $\leftarrow * \rightarrow$ where the * represents $x = 3$). Now, if we observe the point at $x = 1$, when x > 1 the particles are moving to the left and when x < 1, the particles are moving to the right (essentially like $\rightarrow * \leftarrow$ where * represents $x = 1$) and so this is clearly a compression where particles are moving towards each other and so the answer is $x = 1$ which is option **B**.

13.A Polarization depends on the <u>second</u> polarizer and so this means that the polarization does not change thus ruling out options B and D. Now, we know that the intensity is given by $I = I_0\cos^2\theta$ [Topic 4.3] and so since the θ value changes, the value of the intensity changes and so the answer is option **A**.

14.C We know that

$$c = f\lambda \text{ and so } f = \frac{c}{\lambda}$$

Now, let us try to find the wavelengths in both the cases in terms of the length of the pipe. When the pipe is open at both ends, the wavelength is $\lambda = 2L$ and when the pipe is open from only one end is $\lambda = 4L$ for first order harmonic motion as shown in the diagram below:

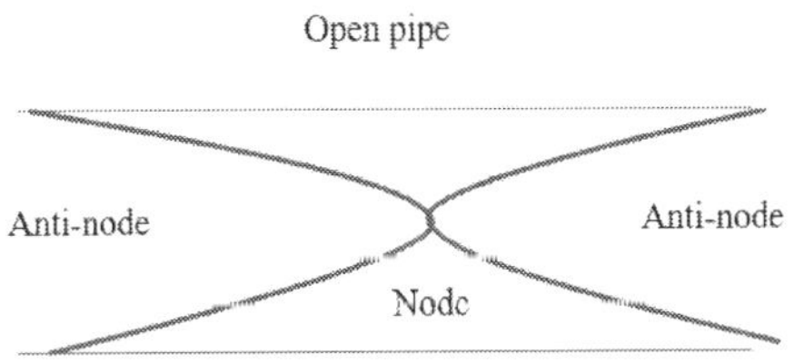

Fundamental - First harmonic

$\lambda = 2L$

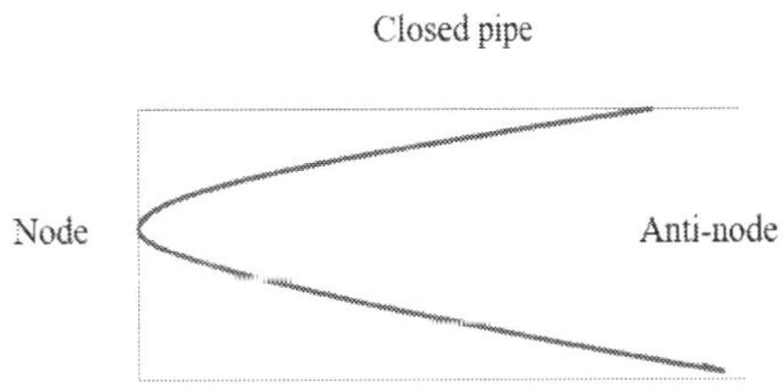

Fundamental - First harmonic

$\lambda = 4L$

And so, since the wavelength is 2 times more in the closed pipe, the frequency (given by $f = \frac{c}{\lambda}$) will be two times less which means that the frequency is 100Hz which is option **C**.

15.B Remember that electric field strength is the force that would be exerted on a small unit positive charge placed at that point. Hence, let us assume that a positive test charge is placed at point S. The resultant force acting on the positive charge:

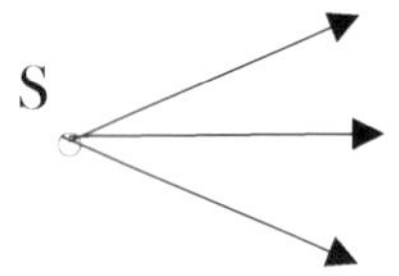

There is no net force acting on S upwards or downwards since the repulsion force caused by the positive charge on the top part of the semi-circular plastic rod balances the repulsion force caused by the positive charge on the bottom part of the semi-circular plastic rod. Hence, from the above diagram it is clear that the resultant force acts in the right direction.
Therefore, the answer is **B.**

16.B Since point X and Y are in series connection, the magnitude of current passing through X and Y are the same (quite intuitive!)

We know that

$$I = nAvq$$

We can see that cross-sectional area and drift speed have an inverse relationship when number of electrons per unit volume, charge of electron and magnitude of current are constant (which is true in this question). As the cross-sectional area doubles at point Y, drift speed halves. Therefore, the answer is **B.**

17.A This question involves the application of Fleming's left-hand rule. The direction of magnetic field (pointer finger) is into the page and the direction of force is upwards (thumb). If we apply Fleming's left-hand rule using these directions, we will figure out that the direction of conventional current is to the right. Since the particle is moving in the same direction as conventional current (when it first enters the magnetic field), the particle must also have the same charge as conventional current. This is because conventional current flows as positive particles. Since the charge of the particle is positive, and thus the particle is an alpha particle. Therefore, the answer is option **A.**

18.D At the very top of the circle (Let's call it position Y)

$$E_p = mgh = W \times 2R$$

$$E_k = \frac{1}{2}mv^2 = \frac{1}{2}WR$$

since centripetal force = $\frac{mv^2}{R}$ and centripetal force = weight (at position Y)
At position X, the ball only has kinetic energy and no potential energy. Thus, according to conservation of energy:
Kinetic energy of the ball at position X = Kinetic energy of the ball at position Y + Potential energy of the ball at position Y

$$E_k\,(minimum\ KE\ at\ position\ X) = 2WR + \frac{1}{2}WR = \frac{5}{2}WR$$

Therefore, the answer is **D.**

19.A A gravitational field strength of 0 at P implies that the magnitude of attractive force on acting on the Earth equals the magnitude of attractive force acting on the moon at point P (eventually leading to cancellation of forces and 0 gravitational field strength)
The first equation:

$$F = \frac{GMm}{r^2}$$

$$F_{Earth} = F_{Moon}$$

$$\frac{GM_{Earth}m}{X^2} = \frac{GM_{Moon}m}{(D - X)^2}$$

$$\frac{M_{Earth}}{X^2} = \frac{M_{Moon}}{(D - X)^2}$$

$$\frac{M_{Moon}}{M_{Earth}} = \frac{(D - X)^2}{X^2}$$

Therefore, the answer is **A.**

20.C We know that

$$Total\ energy = Binding\ energy\ per\ nucleon\ \times\ number\ of\ nucleons$$

$$= 6 \times 11$$

$$= 66\ MeV$$

Therefore, the answer is **C.**

21.C For energy to be released, we need the masses of the products to be lower than the masses of the reactants and so this rules out options A and B. Moreover, for energy to be released we need the binding energy of the products to be more than the binding energy of the reactants because energy is needed to break up the reactants and energy is given out while forming the products, so we need $energy\ neeeded < energy\ given\ out$ and so this gives us option **C** to be the right answer.

22.B The baryon number on the reactant side is 2 (p and n) while the baryon number on the product side is 1 (only p) and so baryon number is not conserved which means that option **B** is the correct answer.

23.A **[Remember]** The main role of a moderator in a nuclear fission reactor is to slow down neutrons. Slowing down the neutrons makes them more effective in the fission chain reaction. The fission chain reaction will continue at a constant rate. Therefore, the answer is **A.**

24.D The loss of energy can be found out by calculating the difference between the energy absorbed from the room and the energy released by the object:

$$energy\ loss = energy\ released - energy\ absorbed$$

And so, we use the formula $P = e\sigma AT^4$ [Topic 8.2] to get the respective values. First, when the temperature is at 400K:

$$energy\ loss = e\sigma A(400)^4 - e\sigma A(300)^4$$

Now, when the temperature is 500K:

$$energy\ loss = e\sigma A(500)^4 - e\sigma A(300)^4$$

By calculating the ratio of energy loss when temperature is 500K and 400K:

$$\frac{loss\ at\ 500K}{loss\ at\ 400K} = \frac{e\sigma A(500)^4 - e\sigma A(300)^4}{e\sigma A(400)^4 - e\sigma A(300)^4} = \frac{500^4 - 300^4}{400^4 - 300^4} = \frac{5^4 - 3^4}{4^4 - 3^4}$$

And so, we can find the loss at 500K to be:

$$loss\ at\ 500K = \frac{5^4 - 3^4}{4^4 - 3^4} \cdot (loss\ at\ 400K) = \frac{5^4 - 3^4}{4^4 - 3^4} \cdot P$$

Therefore, the correct answer is option **D.**

25.D **[Memorize]** Atomic spectra leads to a paradigm shift (an important breakthrough) as it provided evidence of the quantization of energy (energy is thought of occurring in discreet packets called photons) which laid foundation for quantum physics (a major branch in physics). Therefore, the answer is **D.**

Important note: One or two absurd questions like this will pop up in every paper 1, so do read the Nature of Science section in the physics book

---

26.C We know that

$$E_k = \frac{1}{2}m\omega^2({x_0}^2 - x^2)$$

Substituting displacement $= \frac{x_0}{2}$ in the first equation

$$E_k = \frac{1}{2}m\omega^2\left({x_0}^2 - \left(\frac{x_0}{2}\right)^2\right)$$

$$= \frac{3}{4} \times \frac{1}{2} \times m\omega^2({x_0}^2)$$

$$= \frac{3}{4} \times E_t\ (total\ energy)$$

where $E_t = \frac{1}{2} \times m\omega^2({x_0}^2)$

$E_t = 16J$ (Given in the question) and so,

$$E_k = \frac{1}{2} \times 16 = 12J$$

Therefore, the answer is **C.**

27.D We know that

$$s\ (band\ width) = \frac{\lambda D}{d}$$

where D is the distance between the slits and the screen and d is the distance between the slits.

Red light has a higher wavelength when compared to blue light, so λ will increase leading to higher band width. In order to keep the lines of constructive interference in the same position, either the value of D (distance between the slits and the screen) should decrease or the value of d (distance between the slits) should increase (to counter the increase in λ and keep s constant). Moving the slits further apart (option D) refers to an increase in d (distance between the slits), which is the additional change to keep the lines of constructive interference in the same position. Therefore, the answer is **D.**

28.C We know that

$$\theta_D = 1.22\frac{\lambda}{b}$$

For a circular slit, resolution is possible when:

$$\frac{s}{d} \geq 1.22\frac{\lambda}{b}$$

From the above equation, we can conclude that lower the value of $1.22\frac{\lambda}{b}$, higher the probability of definite resolution (since the condition will be met easily). A lower value for $1.22\frac{\lambda}{b}$ can be achieved by decreasing the value of λ (wavelength) and increasing the value of b (slit width). Therefore, the answer is **C.**

29.D In doppler effect, for the frequency to reduce we need the relative motion between the source and the observer to be in such a way that the distance between them is increasing every second. This means that they could be moving away from each other increasingly quicker or also coming towards each other at a decreasing speed. Out of all the options given to us, only option **D** portrays a scenario in which the train (source) is moving away from the observer at increasing speed. Thus, **D** is the correct answer.

30.B We know that work is only done when moving from one equipotential line to another and there are three possibilities given. Using the formula

$$W = Q\Delta V_e$$

You can clearly see that X does the most work as it is moving to the innermost equipotential line (i.e., it passes two equipotentials) while Y and Z only reach the middle equipotential line and therefore do the same amount of work that is lesser than the work done by X. The greater number of equipotential lines you move, the higher is the potential difference. Therefore, we know that the correct answer is option **B.**

31.B At the surface, the potential is V_1 and at a distance of $6R$ it is V_2. We know that the formula for work done in a gravitational field is

$$W = -m\Delta V_g$$

Keep in mind that V_2 is greater than V_1 since V_1 is more negative than V_2. Therefore, we get

$$W = -m(V_2 - V_1)$$
$$W = m(V_1 - V_2)$$

This is option **B.**

32.C Quite simply we use the formula for escape speed from the data booklet

By substituting each of the options given in the question, we can find that option **C** gives the smallest escape speed.

33.B This experiment is quite similar to moving a magnet inside a coil, and so we use Lenz's law here which states that the direction of induced magnetic field is such that it opposes the change causing it. Therefore, when the magnet moves into the ring, the ring moves away to the left and when the magnet moves away from the ring, the rings moves away to the right. This leads us to option **B.**

34.A We know that the magnitude of the induced emf can be calculated by

$$\varepsilon = BvL$$

From the question, we understand that the velocity of all the three different loops are the same and they are moving in the same magnetic field (so same B). Therefore, the strength of the emf depends on the length of the coil. From the image, we can see that the loop Z has the largest length and therefore it will have the largest induced emf, therefore the answer is **A.**

35.C Here we see that two capacitors are connected in series and each of them have a different capacitance. Voltage going through a capacitor depends on its capacitance as shown by

$$C = \frac{q}{V}$$

Since the capacitors are connected in series, the current flowing through them is the same and the charge flowing through them is the same as well. However, the voltage depends on the capacitance and so there will be a different voltage on the two separate capacitors. This leads us to option **C** being the current answer.

36.A This question just requires us to look at the two formulas given in the data booklet regarding the discharge of a capacitor

$$q = q_0 e^{-\frac{t}{\tau}}$$

$$I = I_0 e^{-\frac{t}{\tau}}$$

From both these equations, we can see that the charge and current are both decreasing exponentially, and so option **A** is the correct answer.

37.C This question talks about the energy of electrons emitted, thus we use

$$E_{max} = hf - \phi$$

Increasing the intensity does not make any change to any of the variables in the above equation, and so we can only increase the energy of electrons by increasing the frequency of light and reducing the work function of the metal. This leads us to option **C** being the right answer.

38.A We know that the repulsive/attractive force can be calculated using Coulomb's law

$$F = \frac{kq_1q_2}{r^2}$$

This force is equal to the centripetal force that keeps the electrons in the orbit. Equating the two

$$\frac{kq_1q_2}{r^2} = \frac{mv^2}{r}$$

We get

$$v^2 = \frac{kq_1q_2}{mr}$$

Since in this scenario k,q_1 and q_2 are constants we realize that

$$v \propto \frac{1}{\sqrt{r}}$$

From this inverse relationship, when r increases to 4r, v will decrease to $\frac{v}{2}$ and this gives us the answer as **A.**

39.A Let us approach the question using the units method and we will derive the units of each of the options and see which one corresponds with that of the kinetic energy (J). For the first option: the unit for h is Js, the unit for mass is kg and the unit for diameter is m. Therefore,

$$\frac{h^2}{md^2} = \frac{(Js)^2}{kgm^2} = \frac{J^2}{kgm^2s^{-2}} = \frac{J^2}{kgms^{-2}m}$$

We know that $kgms^{-2}$ is the unit for force while m is the unit for distance and so the quantity in the denominator is $force \times distance = work$ and the unit for work done is Joules. Therefore,

$$\frac{J^2}{kgms^{-2}m} = \frac{J^2}{J} = J$$

Now we know that this formula does lead to the unit of Joules and it can be the formula for the kinetic energy. The only way to be sure that this is the correct answer is to check that the units for the remaining options do not lead to Joules. You can try this by yourself and you will realize that the units for:

Option B is $Jskgm^{-1}$

Option C is kgJ^2sm^{-2}

Option D is $Jskg^{-2}m^{-1}$

Therefore, the correct answer is option **A.**

40.A For this question we will use the formula from the data booklet

$$N = N_0e^{-\lambda t}$$

and N is the number of atoms remaining at time t. At $t = 0$

$$N = N_0$$

If $t = 1$

$$N = N_0e^{-\lambda}$$

If we find the difference between the two, we get

$$N_0(1 - e^{-\lambda})$$

Keep in mind that N_0 signifies the initial number of nuclei and for this particular question that value is actually N. Therefore, we can see that the answer is **A.**

1.C The value of the charge of an electron is $1.6 \times 10^{-19}C$ which is the same as $1.6 \times 10^{-22}kC$ as one kC is 10^3C. Therefore, the correct answer is option **C.**

2.B **[Memorize]** The use of the light behind the pointer is to reduce the risk of parallax error. This is because when your eye is in the correct position, the reflection of the pointer is hidden behind the pointer itself. If you can see the reflection, it means you are looking at an angle and will record a wrong reading. Therefore, the correct answer is option **B.**

3.D Acceleration is constant (at $9.81m/s^2$) for any object regardless of what height the object is released. This makes option **D** the correct answer. Option A is the wrong answer because the object has an initial motion upwards and the object moves a small distance up until the velocity becomes 0. Therefore, in the second case, the distance travelled by the object is greater than h.

4.C The weight of the object is acting downwards, there is friction between the block and the slope and there is a normal reaction force acting at 90 degrees. The below diagram shows the scenario:

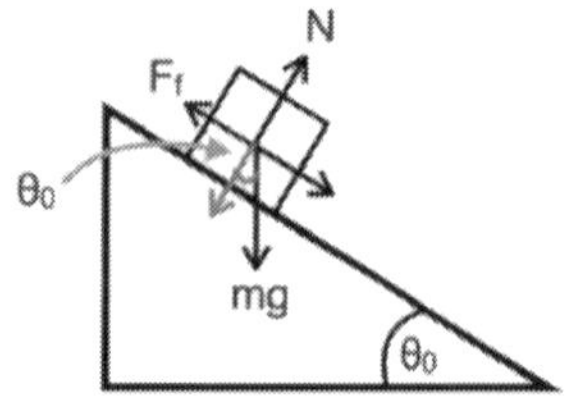

(this diagram is an inverted image of the one in the question)

The component of mg that is perpendicular to the plane of the slope is the value of normal reaction which is

$$mgcos\theta$$

The component of mg that is parallel to the plane of the slope is equal to the value of frictional force which is $\mu_s mgsin\theta$ and thus equating the two we have

$$mgcos\theta = \mu_s mgsin\theta$$

Simplifying this, we get

$$\mu_s = \frac{sin\theta}{cos\theta}$$

So, the coefficient of static friction is $tan\theta$ and therefore, the correct answer is option **C.**

5.D The sum of the forces acting upward and downward must be balanced (equal to each other) so that the sunbather is supported. This only happens in the diagram in option **D** and so that is the correct answer.

6.B We know that the extension is half of the initial extension because there are two springs instead of one. This is because $F = kx$ and so $x = \frac{F}{k}$ and now the force is split equally in half between the two springs. The formula for elastic potential energy is $E = \frac{1}{2}kx^2$ and so since x becomes $\frac{x}{2}$ the energy reduces by a factor of 4 for each spring. This means that the total elastic potential energy stored is $\frac{E}{4} + \frac{E}{4} = \frac{E}{2}$ and therefore, the correct answer is option **B**.

7.A Impulse is the same as change in momentum. The initial momentum is $0.15 \times 0.1 = 0.015$ and the final momentum is $0.15 \times 0.15 = 0.0225$. The difference is $0.0225 - 0.015$ is $0.0075 = 7.5 \times 10^{-3} = 7.5\ mN\ s$ which is option **A**.

8.B We know that

$$P = \frac{E}{t} \text{ and } E = mc\Delta T$$

The energy gained is $0.5 \times 4000 \times 80 = 160{,}000J$ and the corresponding power is $\frac{160{,}000}{200} = 800W.$ The heater supplies 1000W of power and so the total power lost is $1000 - 800 = 200W$, and so, the answer is option **B**.

9.B Solids have the least internal energy and gases have the most internal energy. The amount of vibration in the three states are similar (but solids have the highest vibration) and so this means that the ratio of energy from molecular vibration to energy is highest in solids, then liquids and lowest in gases. Therefore, the correct answer is option **B**.

10.B **[Memorize]** In the formula, $pV = nRT$, n is the number of moles of the gas. So, the correct answer is option **B**.

11.B At maximum displacement (amplitude), the velocity is 0 and when the displacement is 0, the velocity is maximum according to SHM.
Note: velocity is just the differentiation of displacement
Therefore, the correct answer is option **B.**

12.D When the light passes through the first filter, the intensity becomes half of the initial intensity $\left(\frac{I_0}{2}\right)$. After that the intensity is calculated by $I = I_0\cos^2\theta = \frac{I_0}{2}\left(\frac{\sqrt{3}}{2}\right)^2 = \frac{3}{8}I_0$ and therefore, the answer is option **D**.

13.A By using the ratio method, we know that since the refractive index from X to Y is $\frac{4}{3}$ the index of X is 4 and the index of Y is 3 (in its simplest form). Since the refractive index from Y to Z is $\frac{3}{5}$, the index of Y is 3 and the index of Z is 5. Therefore, the refractive index from X to Z is $\frac{4}{5}$ which is option **A.**

14.A Phase difference is used to describe the difference in degrees or radians when two or more alternating quantities reach their maximum or zero values. Phase difference is a way of expressing how in 'step' two particles are. Particles X and Y are both at an equal height on the diagram. Because this is a standing wave, X any Y will continue to move up and down at the same time. So, their phase difference remains at 0, thereby making option **A** the correct answer.

15.A Let the radius of wire X be $2x$ and let the radius of wire Y be x. The formula for drift velocity is $v = \frac{I}{neA}$ and so since I, n and e are same for both X and Y, the only thing affecting the ratio is A. The area of X is $\pi(2x)^2$ and the area of Y is $\pi(x)^2$ and so the ratio is:

$$\frac{\frac{I}{ne\pi(2x)^2}}{\frac{I}{ne\pi(x)^2}} = \frac{\frac{1}{\pi(2x)^2}}{\frac{1}{\pi(x)^2}} = \frac{1}{\pi(2x)^2} \times \frac{\pi(x)^2}{1} = \frac{\pi x^2}{4\pi x^2} = \frac{1}{4}$$

Therefore, the correct answer is option **A.**

16.B The voltage law states that in a closed loop of d.c. current, the algebraic sum of the p.d and e.m.f. is always zero. When analyzing a loop, if there is a rise in voltage then that is taken as positive and a fall in voltage is taken as negative.

When you move with the direction of the current that means you will have a voltage drop across the resistor. Let us calculate the total voltage using the above rules and sum it to 0: $-3I_2 + 4I_3 = 0$ which can be written as $0 = 3I_2 - 4I_3$. Therefore, option **B** is the correct answer.
Note: when you move from negative terminal to positive terminal there is a voltage lift (positive voltage). When you move from positive terminal to negative terminal there is a voltage drop.

17.A This question tests our understanding of Fleming's left-hand rule. (In fact, we think that this is a very complicated way of asking a very simple question). Let us ignore the presence of wire P in the question as that is present only to trick candidates into complicating the question. We can simply apply Fleming's left hand rule where our middle finger goes left to right and we can see that the thumb is pointing upwards and so this makes option **A** the correct answer.

18.B Using the right-hand grip rule, where the fingers curling represents the curving magnetic field we can see that the conventional current flow direction is out of the page for P and into the page for Q. This means that the electron flow (which is opposite to conventional current flow) is into the page for P and out of the page for Q and so the answer is option **B.**

19.B **[Memorize]** The mass of satellite (or orbiting body) does not affect the orbital period and so the correct answer is option **B.**
Note: however, do remember that the mass of the planet does affect the orbital period

---

20.D The emission lines may sometimes correspond to ultraviolet radiation or infra-red radiation, so it is not always in visible light range. Therefore, the correct answer is option **D.**

21.B Since nuclear fusion releases energy, which is caused by the mass that has been lost from the reactants while forming the products, the nuclear mass of the products reduces. Nuclear fusion results in the formation of heavier nuclei which have higher binding energy per nucleon and so, the binding energy of the products increases. Therefore, the correct answer is option **B**.

22.C Since time is increasing from bottom to top, the two particles interacting are X and Y which result in the formation of U and Z. Therefore, option **C** is the correct answer.

23.D From the formula

$$A = \lambda N_0 e^{-\lambda t}$$

we know that λ (decay constant) and N_0 is constant. And so, this means that the graph is in the same shape as a e^{-x} graph which looks like the graphs in option A and D. However, option A is wrong because half life and activity can never be 0 and so this means that option **D** is the correct answer.

24.C Sun and biomass are renewable sources of energy whereas crude oil and coil are non-renewable sources. Therefore, the correct answer is option **C** where the renewable energy is biomass while non-renewable energy is crude oil.

25.B We know that

$$\lambda_{max} T = b$$

where b is a constant and so $\lambda_{max} = \frac{b}{T}$ which means that if T doubles, then the peak wavelength halves. This makes option **B** the correct answer.

26.A The solar constant mainly depends on how far the earth is from the sun and the tilt of the earth does not affect the solar constant. Obviously, the power output of the sun varying is a valid reason for using an average value. Therefore, the correct answer is option **A**.

27.B We know the formula

$$E = \frac{1}{2}m\omega^2 x^2$$

where x is maximum displacement. We also know that $\omega = 2\pi f = \frac{2\pi}{T}$. Since mass triples, and we know that $T = 2\pi\sqrt{\frac{m}{k}}$, it means that time period increases by a factor of $\sqrt{3}$ which means that ω reduces by a factor of $\sqrt{3}$ and so this means ω^2 reduces by a factor of 3 which balances the increase in mass by a factor of 3. Therefore, the only aspect that affects the energy is the change in displacement. The displacement increases by a factor of 2 which means that x^2 (and thus E) increases by a factor of 4. Therefore, the correct answer is option **B.**

28.A When one slit is covered, the double slit experiment changes into a single slit experiment. It has some effects on the observed pattern on the screen:

1. There is greater diffraction and so the light-bands will have larger length
2. The intensity reduces
3. Fewer maxima will be observed

Therefore, the only one of the above points are mentioned in the question and that is the point about fewer maxima which is option **A.**

29.A There is a phase change of π upon reflection from a denser medium and no phase change upon reflection from a rarer medium. Since the layer of film is denser than air, light waves that get reflected from surface of film (denser medium) to the air undergo phase change. In this case, that is only line **J** and so the correct answer is option **A.**

30.A The speed does not change when the source moves away, however the wavelength does change. From the formula for frequency when the source moves away, we know that the frequency reduces. Since, the frequency reduces (and speed remains same), the wavelength must increase because of the formula $v = f\lambda$ and therefore, the correct answer is option **A.**

31.C No matter what path a charged object takes in the field, if the charge returns to its starting point, the net amount of work is zero. The formula to calculate the work done while moving from A to B is $W = Q \cdot \Delta V = 3 \times (10 - (-20)) = 3 \times 30 = 90$ and so the correct answer is option **C.**

32.C The formula for gravitation potential energy is

$$E = -\frac{GMm}{r}$$

the formula for gravitational field strength is $g = -\frac{GM}{r^2}$ and the formula for gravitation force is $F = \frac{GMm}{r^2}$ and from this we can see that only g and F are proportional to $\frac{1}{r^2}$. Therefore, the correct answer is option **C.**

33.B Inside the metal sphere, the electric potential remains constant (Obviously, since the electric field inside the sphere is zero, there is no force on the charge, so no work done). As we move outside the metal sphere, we can find the potential using the formula $V = \frac{kq}{r} = \frac{kq}{x}$ and so as x increases, V decreases and this matches the graph in option **B** which is the correct answer.

34.D We know that

$$\varepsilon = -N\frac{\Delta\phi}{\Delta t}$$

and we also know that $\phi = BA$ ($\theta = 0$, so $cos\theta = 1$). Therefore, we can derive that $\varepsilon = \frac{NBA}{t}$. Notice that the coil is only making half a rotation during time t, therefore the induced emf is twice what it would be if the coil made one full rotation in time t. Therefore, in this case, $\varepsilon = \frac{2NBA}{t}$, which matches option **D.**

35.C We know the formula that

$$\frac{N_P}{N_S} = \frac{V_P}{V_S}$$

and so substituting values into the equation we get:

$$2.5 = \frac{200}{V_S} \text{ and so } V_S = \frac{200}{2.5} = 80.$$

Using the formula $P = VI$ we know that the input power in primary coil is $0.25 \times 200 = 50W$ and the corresponding value for the secondary coil is $0.5 \times 80 = 40W$. Efficiency can be calculated by the formula

$$Efficiency = \frac{useful\,power\,out}{total\,power\,in} = \frac{40}{50} = 0.8$$

and therefore, the answer is option **C.**

36.B We know that

$$T = \frac{1}{f}$$

and so, if frequency doubles, the time period will become half of the original value. We also know that peak emf, $\varepsilon_0 = NBA\omega = NBA2\pi f$ which tells us that ε_0 is directly proportional to frequency and so if frequency doubles then peak emf is doubled as well. Therefore, the correct answer is option **B.**

37.B In this question, we have one group of 3 capacitors in series connected in parallel with another group of 3 capacitors in series. The total capacitance for the series is given by:

$$\frac{1}{C_{total}} = \frac{1}{C} + \frac{1}{C} + \frac{1}{C} = \frac{3}{C}$$

So, we know that the total capacitance is $\frac{3}{C}$ and then we can add up the two groups connected in the formula using:

$$C_{total} = \frac{C}{3} + \frac{C}{3} = \frac{2C}{3}$$

which is option **B** and that is the correct answer.

38.B The resistance and capacitance both double and so this increases the time constant of the circuit. Therefore, this means that the time taken for the capacitor to discharge half its initial value is increased. So, the correct answer is option **B.**

39.C It is much easier to remove the electrons that are on the surface of the metal rather than the electrons that are deeper inside. Therefore, the kinetic energy of the electrons differ and so the correct answer is option **C.**

40.B **[Memorize]** Pair production is the process in which a photon reacts with a nearby nucleus to produce an electron. Therefore, option **B** is the correct answer.

1.B The volume of a sphere is given by the formula

$$V = \frac{4}{3}\pi r^3$$

The uncertainty in the volume is

$$\frac{\Delta V}{V} = 3\frac{\Delta r}{r}$$

This is because for an equation

$$y = a^n$$

The fractional uncertainty is always

$$\frac{\Delta y}{y} = n\left(\frac{\Delta a}{a}\right)$$

Therefore, the answer is **B.**

2.A The displacement of the object at times 2s and 8s are the same. The object is being acted with acceleration of $10m/s^2$ downwards so we must take acceleration of negative value. The formula for displacement is

$$s = ut + \frac{1}{2}at^2$$

Subbing in the value of $t = 2$ and $t = 8$ we get

$$2u - 5(2)^2 = 8u - 5(8)^2$$

The above 2 displacements are equated as the object is in the same position at those respective times. Therefore, we get

$$6u = 5(64 - 4)$$

$$6u = 5(60)$$

$$u = 50m/s$$

So, the answer is **A.**

3.B Since the ground is rough, the ladder is acted upon by friction from the ground which acts rightwards (since the ladder wishes to move left as it can slide down from the wall). The wall has no friction on the ladder which is why there is no upward force acting on the ladder that opposes the tendency of the ladder to move down (slide down). And in both cases there is a normal reaction force that acts perpendicularly from the surface (the ground and the wall). This leads us to option **B** being the right answer.

4.A When object is at rest, it only has gravitational potential energy and no kinetic energy. As the object falls down, some of the GPE converts to KE. At a height of h/4 above the surface, the object has fallen 3h/4. Therefore, from an amount of

$$GPE = mgh$$

When it is at a height of h, it falls to

$$GPE = mg\left(\frac{h}{4}\right)$$

when the height is h/4. Therefore, the difference in GPE is

$$\frac{3mgh}{4}$$

Which has been converted into kinetic energy. So, the ratio will be

$$\frac{\frac{3mgh}{4}}{mgh}$$

Which is simply ¾, thus leading to **A** as the correct answer.

5.D **[Memorize]** The law of conservation of momentum states that the total momentum of a closed system remains unchanged. Therefore, option **D** is the right answer.

6.D Since the parachute is travelling at constant speed, it means that he has 0 acceleration and has 0 net force. The earth's gravity is pulling him with a force of 700N ($70kg \cdot 10m/s^2$). Therefore, for net force to be equal to 0, the force of air resistance pushing him upwards must equal 700N, leading to option **D** being the right answer.

7.C We can calculate the force using the formula

$$F = ma$$

To find the acceleration, we use the formula

$$a = \frac{(v - u)}{t}$$

Acceleration is therefore equal to

$$\frac{20}{1.6 \times 10^{-3}}$$

Which is $1250\ m/s^2$. So now the total force can be obtained by multiplying the mass (8×10^{-3}kg) with the acceleration, thus giving us 10N. Therefore, **C** is the right answer.

8.C The unit for specific heat capacity can be derived by using the units in the formula of

$$c = \frac{Q}{m\Delta T} = J/kgK$$

The specific latent heat can be found by the formula

$$L = \frac{Q}{m} = J/kg$$

So, we simply divide the two

$$\frac{J/kgK}{J/kg} = \frac{J}{kgK} \times \frac{kg}{J} = K^{-1}$$

This gives us K^{-1} as the unit of the ratio and so, option **C** is the right answer.

9.D We know the formula

$$pV = NRT$$

And so,

$$p = \frac{nRT}{V}$$

We also know that number of moles, n, can be shown as

$$n = \frac{N}{N_A}$$

where N is number of particles in substance and N_A is the Avogadro's constant. From here we can rewrite the equation as

$$p = \frac{N\left(\frac{R}{N_A}\right)T}{V}$$

Volume is simply the product of circular surface area and length of cylinder. Replacing that in the above equation

$$p = \frac{N\left(\frac{R}{N_A}\right)T}{Al}$$

Since force is pressure times area, the area in the denominator gets cancelled:

$$F = \frac{N\left(\frac{R}{N_A}\right)T}{l}$$

We know that

$$\left(\frac{R}{N_A}\right) = K_B$$

Therefore, this simplifies to

$$F = \frac{NK_BT}{l}$$

This gives us option **D** to be the right answer.

10.A Pressure is directly proportional to temperature and the pressure at $0°C$ is the same as pressure at 273K (and this pressure is not equal to 0 which means that the answer cannot be C). Therefore, option **A** is the right answer.

11.D For a string that is closed end and open at one end, the distance between 2 nodes is

$$\frac{\lambda}{4}$$

We know that

$$\frac{\lambda}{4} = 3$$

And so $\lambda = 12m$. We can find speed using the formula

$$v = f\lambda$$

Therefore, the speed of the wave is 3600m/s and so the correct answer is **D**.

12.D By observing the graph, we can see that one of the waves is $\pi/2$ ahead in terms of phase and so that would be 90°. Using the principle of superposition at $t = 2.0ms$, we can clearly see that one wave is at $-1.6mm$ and the other wave is at $1mm$ and so the vector sum of the two is $-0.6mm$. This leads us to the conclusion that option **D** is correct.

13.A For total internal reflection, the incident angle has to be more than the critical angle and so we need θ to increase as a smaller angle would mean total internal reflection cannot happen. The aforementioned way of causing total internal reflection is by increasing angle of incidence but it can also be done by decreasing critical angle which is calculated by

$$\sin(critical\ angle) = \frac{1}{n}$$

So, to reduce critical angle, we have to increase n. Therefore, option **A** is the correct answer.

14.B **[Memorize]** In simple harmonic motion, the restoring force on the object is opposite and directly proportional to the displacement of the object. So, the answer is **B**.

15.C We know that

$$\Delta V = \frac{W}{q}$$

which can also be written as $\Delta V = \frac{Fs}{q}$ and then further simplified to $\Delta V = \frac{Eqs}{q}$ as $F = Eq$ **[Topic 5.1]**. Therefore, the answer is just $\Delta V = Es$ which is option **C**.

16.A The two 3Ω resistors are connected in series, so their total resistance is 6Ω. The points X and Y are such that the effective resistance between the two resistors in series is parallel to the 2Ω resistors (in other words, an imaginary 6Ω resistor is parallel to the 2 Ω resistor). Therefore, the total resistance would be,

$$\frac{1}{R} = \frac{1}{6} + \frac{1}{2} = \frac{4}{6}$$

And so $R = \frac{6}{4}$ which is 1.5Ω so option **A** is the correct answer.

17.C We know that $E = 4R \cdot I$ and so

$$I = \frac{E}{4R}$$

The power can then be calculated to be

$$P_{initial} = I^2 \cdot 4R = \left(\frac{E}{4R}\right)^2 \cdot 4R = \frac{E^2}{4R} = P$$

With a resistance of R, the corresponding I would be $\frac{E}{R}$ and so the power could be

$$P_{new} = I^2 R = \frac{E^2}{R^2} \cdot R = \frac{E^2}{R} = 4\left(\frac{E^2}{4R}\right) = 4P$$

Therefore, we can see that this is 4 times the initial power dissipated and so the amount of power dissipated with resistance R would be $4P$, making option **C** the correct answer.

18.A We know that $a = \omega^2 r$ [*Topic* 9.1] and thus $F = ma = m\omega^2 r$. The resultant force for this object undergoing centripetal force would be $T - mg$ since T is acting upwards and mg is acting downwards. Therefore, if we equate the two: $m\omega^2 r = T - mg$ we would get $T = m(\omega^2 r + g)$
and so, the answer would be option **A**.

19.A The equation for a B^+ decay is $u \rightarrow d + e^{+1} + \nu_e$ which is the diagram shown in option **A.**

20.C By multiplying the binding energy per nucleon with the number of nucleons in the atom, we get $7.5 \cdot 15 = 112.5 MeV$ which is close to $113 MeV$ and so the answer is **C.**

21.A **[Memorize]** The Higgs Boson was predicted before it was observed. Therefore, the answer is option **A.**

22.B The formula for specific energy is E/m while for energy density it is E/V where V is the volume of the object. Therefore, the ratio would be

$$\frac{\frac{E}{m}}{\frac{E}{V}} = \frac{E}{m} \cdot \frac{V}{E} = \frac{V}{m} = \frac{1}{\frac{m}{V}} = \frac{1}{density}$$

and so, the answer is option **B.**

23.B **[Memorize]** The purpose of the moderator atoms is to slow down the neutrons but not to absorb them, while the purpose of the control atoms is to absorb the neutrons in order to reduce the number of neutrons in the reactor. So, the correct answer is **B.**

24.A We don't necessarily need the graph to answer the question. Just **[Memorize]** The greenhouse effect is a phenomenon where the Sun's radiation at the <u>infrared</u> frequency can enter the Earth's atmosphere but cannot leave it, as it is absorbed by (mainly) Oxygen and Nitrogen, leading to a net heating effect.

The option which highlights the absorption of infrared is **A.**

25.A We know that

$$Albedo = \frac{scattered}{total} = \frac{6 + 4 + 20}{100} = \frac{30}{100} = 0.3$$

and so, the answer is **A.**

26.B We know that

$$T = 2\pi\sqrt{\frac{l}{g}}$$

for a simple pendulum so as g decreases, the T increases. For a mass-spring system $T = 2\pi\sqrt{\frac{m}{k}}$ and this is independent of g which means T does not change. Therefore, the answer is **B**.

27.C Since this is a minimum, we know it is a destructive interference and so the formula is

$$2dn = m\lambda$$

And so, for $d = \frac{m\lambda}{2n} = \frac{m}{2}\left(\frac{\lambda}{n}\right)$ where m is an integer, the only option that mathematically fits the equation is option **C** as all the other options need a value of m that is not an integer. Thus, option **C** is the correct answer.

28.C We know the formula $b\sin\theta = \lambda$ **[Topic 9.2]** where b is the width of the slit. Since the width of the slit does not change (and λ doesn't change), the angle does not change. This rules out options A, B and D. Moreover, we know that the peak intensity is proportional to the square of the number of slits illuminated. Increasing the number of slits not only makes the diffraction maximum sharper, but also much more intense (and hence brighter). Also note that an increase in number of slits leads to decrease in the width of the maxima. Therefore, the correct answer is option **C**.

29.C We know that

$$\frac{\Delta\lambda}{\lambda} = \frac{v}{c}$$

and so $\Delta\lambda = \lambda \cdot \frac{v}{c}$ which means that when the observer moves away, the shift for Y will be a lot more than the shift for X since X has a lower wavelength than Y. This is represented in the diagram in option **C**.

30.D The potential is given by the formula

$$V = \frac{kQ}{r}$$

and we need to calculate r using Pythagoras theorem: $(2r)^2 = (2d)^2 + (2d)^2$ and so we get $r = \sqrt{2}d$. Therefore, for one charge the potential is $V = \frac{kQ}{\sqrt{2}d}$ and we multiply that by 4 to accommodate for 4 charges to get $V = \frac{4kQ}{\sqrt{2}d}$ which can be written as $V = \frac{2\sqrt{2}kQ}{d}$ which is option **D**.

31.D Objects tend to move towards the lower potential which means that this mass will move towards the left. Moreover, $g = \frac{\Delta V}{\Delta d}$ and so as d decreases, the value of g increases which means that the acceleration will be more. This leads to option **D** being the correct answer.

32.A By equating the electrical force with centripetal force, we have:

$$\frac{k \cdot e \cdot 2e}{r^2} = \frac{mv^2}{r}$$

and so, we get

$$v^2 = \frac{2ke^2}{m}$$

which eventually leads to

$$v = \sqrt{\frac{2ke^2}{mr}}$$

and thus, option **A** is correct.

33.C Let's use the following references for ease of explanation
The circular coil connected to a cell and switch: coil A
The coil below coil A: coil B

As the switch is closing, there is an increase in the magnitude of current passing through coil A. Increase in current leads to an increase in magnetic field, which induces current in coil B. Lenz's law states that an induced electric current flows in a direction such that the current opposes the change that induced it. When the switch is closed, the current flows through coil A in anti-clockwise direction (current flows from positive to negative terminal of the cell). Using right hand grip rule, we can figure out that the direction of magnetic field is downwards. Using Lenz law, we can deduce that the direction of current induced in coil B will be such that the magnetic field direction is upwards (opposes the change that produces it). Using right hand grip rule, we can deduce that the direction of current in coil B is clockwise. Moreover, we also know that two coils carrying current in opposite directions repel each other. Since current direction in coil A is anti-clockwise and current direction in coil B is clockwise, there will be a repulsive force between the two coils.

Now let's look at the second scenario: switch is opening. As the switch is opening, there is a decrease in the magnitude of current passing through coil B. Decrease in current leads to decrease in magnetic field, which leads to decrease in flux. If it is decreasing, the induced field acts in the direction of the applied field to oppose the change. So, the current induced in coil B must produce a magnetic field in the same direction as that in coil A (which is downwards). Using right hand grip rule, we can deduce that the direction of the current in coil B is anti-clockwise. Moreover, we also know that two coils carrying current in same directions attract each other. Since current direction in coil A is anti-clockwise and current direction in coil B is also anti-clockwise, there will be an attractive force between the two coils.
Therefore, the answer is **C**.

34.D In a step-up transformer, the voltage is increased in the secondary coil by reducing the amount of current and so this rules out options A and C. Moreover, there is a phase-shift between the current in the primary and the secondary coil and so the answer is option **D**.

35.C We need a capacitor connected in such a way that we keep the voltage constant and so this is done by connecting one resistor in parallel to the cell which is the diagram shown in option **C**.

36.A We know that

$$C = \frac{\varepsilon A}{d}$$

and the $field = \frac{V}{d}$ and so as d increases 2 times, the field strength decreases two times (which means it becomes 50). As for the energy we know the formula is $E = \frac{CV^2}{2}$ and so as d increases two times, the C decreases two times and so the E also decreases two times to 2J as $E \propto C$. Therefore, the answer is **A.**

37.D X undergoes 4 half-lives while Y undergoes 2 half-lives and so the portion of X remaining is $\frac{N}{2^4} = \frac{N}{16}$ and the portion of Y that remains is $\frac{N}{2^2} = \frac{N}{4}$. Therefore,

$$\frac{\frac{N}{16}}{\frac{N}{4}} = \frac{N}{16} \cdot \frac{4}{N} = \frac{4}{16} = \frac{1}{4}$$

and so, the correct answer is **D.**

38.B The emissions that can be recorded are from levels 3,4,5 and so on to level 2. The dotted line is from $n = 3$ to $n = 2$.
The emission from $n = 4$ to $n = 2$ will have a higher energy than the one from $n = 3$ to $n = 2$ which means that it will have a lower wavelength. This applies to emissions from $n = 5$ to $n = 2$ and so on.
Note: this is because $E = \frac{hc}{\lambda}$ and so energy is inversely proportional to wavelength
So, we know that the other lines must be on the left side of the dotted line (because they have higher energy)
This rules out options **C** and **D.** We know the formula

$$E = -\frac{13.6}{n^2}$$

Where n is the shell number. So, as we go to higher shells, the gap between the energy levels of the consecutive shells decrease. For instance, $n = 2 \rightarrow E = -3.4$, $n = 3 \rightarrow E = -1.51$ and $n = 4 \rightarrow E = -0.85$. Therefore, the emission from $n = 4$ to $n = 2$ has much higher energy than the dotted line but it is very close to the emission from $n = 5$ to $n = 2$ because of the closeness of the energy levels in $n = 4$ and $n = 5$. This is not reflected in option A and thus the correct answer is option **B.**

39.D **[Memorize]** The tunneling probability will always be greater when both the width and the height of the tunnel are lower. Therefore, the correct answer is option **D.**

40.B The deviations happen when the alpha particles get very close to the subatomic particles and this only happens when the energy of the alpha particles is very high and there is a low value of Z (which means less positive charge) and so the answer is **B.**

1.C Go to page 1 of your physics data booklet. Look at the approximate value of Fermi radius. The approximate value has the order $10^{-15}m$. Therefore, the answer is **C.** Golden Rule: These kinds of estimate questions are quite common in IB physics paper 1. To prepare for these types of questions, read the first chapter in the Tsokos physics HL textbook. It has 3 tables with different estimates, which will effectively prepare you to tackle such types of questions

---

2.B We know that

$$Efficiency = \frac{Useful\ power\ output}{Total\ power\ input}$$

We also know that

$$Output\ power = F \times v = M \times g \times v = 8 \times 10 \times \frac{1}{2} = 40W$$

Substituting output power as 40W in the first equation:

$$Efficiency = \frac{40}{160} \times 100 = 25\%$$

Therefore, the answer is **B.**

3.D The first thing we should note is that the vertical forces must balance each other, so $F_n\,(normal\ reaction\ force) = F_g(weight)$. This rules out options A and B. Since the box is accelerating to the right and not moving at constant speed, forward force (F_a) needs to be greater than the friction force (F_f). Therefore, the answer is **D.**

Important note:

- When a body is moving at constant speed, net resultant force = 0 (forward force = opposing force)
- When a body is accelerating, forward force is greater than the opposing force. The net resultant force (F) is calculated by using the formula $F = ma$
- When a body is decelerating, opposing force is greater than the forward force. The net resultant force (F) is calculated by using the formula $F = ma$

4.B Area under the given graph will give us the change of momentum, which is nothing but impulse.

$$Impulse = \frac{1}{2} \times 6000 \times 30 = 90000\ Ns$$

Impulse is the change in momentum

$$m(v - u) = 90000$$

$u = 0$ since the object initially starts from rest

$$mv = 90000$$

And $m = 15000\ kg$

$$v\ (final\ velocity) = \frac{90000}{15000} = 6\ ms^{-1}$$

Therefore, the answer is **B.**

Important note: Always remember that the rate of change of momentum is equal to the force. When a question states rate of change of momentum, it is nothing but force

---

5.B At point Q, there is only horizontal component of velocity. So, vertical component of velocity $=$ 0. Note that horizontal component of velocity remains constant during the entire projectile motion (air resistance needs to be negligible, otherwise horizontal component will not remain constant throughout the motion). Horizontal component of velocity $= ucos(\theta)$ (knowing basic trigonometry helps!)

Momentum of the ball at Q = mass of the ball $\times$ horizontal velocity at Q

$$= mucos(\theta)$$

Therefore, the answer is **B.**

Important note: Horizontal component of velocity will not remain constant throughout the motion if air resistance is present. Negligible air resistance is a pre-condition for projectile motion.

6.B The first equation (we are assuming constant acceleration)

$$s = ut + \frac{1}{2}at^2$$

Making acceleration (a) the subject of the first equation

$$a = \frac{s - ut}{0.5t^2}$$

(ball starts from rest, so initial velocity (u) = 0)

There are totally 5 time intervals of $1.0\ ms$, so total time $= 1 \times 5 \times 10^{-3}\ seconds$

$$a = \frac{0.05}{0.5 \times (1 \times 5 \times 10^{-3})^2} = 4000\ ms^{-1}$$

Therefore, the answer is **B.**

Important note: the equations of motion can only be used when acceleration is constant

---

7.D Force is the rate of change of momentum. The rebound time is $t_2 - t_1$ (since the ball hits the wall at time t_1 and bounces off the ball at t_2).

Change of momentum $= mu - (-mv)$ (after bouncing, the velocity is negative since there is a change in direction, so final momentum is $-mv$ not $+mv$)

$$Magnitude\ of\ mean\ force = \frac{\Delta p}{t}$$

$$= \frac{m(u + v)}{t_2 - t_1}$$

Therefore, the answer is **D.**

Important note: Whenever you see a question dealing with bouncing or rebound, remember that the change of momentum is $m(u + v)$ not $m(v - u)$. This is a common mistake that can lead to loss of many marks

8.A We know from Topic 3.1 that

$$q = mc\Delta T$$

Dividing both sides of the equation by time t

$$\frac{q}{t} = \frac{mc\Delta T}{t}$$

Since $Power = \frac{q\ (energy)}{t\ (time)}$, we can replace $\frac{q}{t}$ with P

$$P = \frac{mc\Delta T}{t}$$

The second equation

$$m = \frac{Pt}{c\Delta T}$$

Gradient of the graph (K) $= \frac{\Delta T\ (change\ in\ temperaure)}{\Delta t\ (time)}$, thus $\frac{\Delta t\ (time)}{\Delta T\ (change\ temperature)} = \frac{1}{K}$

Replacing $\frac{\Delta t\ (time)}{\Delta T\ (change\ temperature)}$ with $\frac{1}{K}$ in the second equation

$$m = \frac{P}{cK}$$

Therefore, the answer is **A**

9.A Let us do this question by calculating the product of the pressure and volume (this is a measure of cumulative particle energy – don't worry, you don't need to know this!) in the two containers. The value for container Q is $3Vp$ and the value for container R is $3Vp$ also. The total combined value is $6Vp$. Now, when the valve is opened, both containers share the same pressure, and their combined volume is $4V$. As temperature does not change, we can divide $6Vp$ by the combined volume of $4V$ to get a shared pressure of $1.5p$. For container Q, this represents a

$\frac{p}{2}$ increase

from its initial pressure $(of\ p)$. Therefore, the correct answer is option **B.**

10.D We know that

$$Time = \frac{Distance\ (d)}{Speed}$$

Assume that the wave with speed 7.5 kms^{-1} takes time T_1 and the wave with speed 5.0 kms^{-1} takes time T_2

$$T_1 = \frac{d}{5}$$

$$T_2 = \frac{d}{7.5}$$

It is obvious that T_2 is less than T_1. We know that the waves arrive at the detector 15 seconds apart

$$T_1 - T_2 = 15$$

$$\frac{d}{5} - \frac{d}{7.5} = 15$$

$$d = 225\ km$$

Therefore, the answer is **D**

11.D Let's assume that velocity of the particle in SHM = $-x_0\omega sin(\omega t)$

Now we need to find the acceleration of the particle. We know that acceleration can be found by finding the derivative of the velocity.

Acceleration = $-x_0\omega^2 cos(\omega t)$

When velocity is a sin graph, acceleration will be the cosine graph (derivative of sine) and vice versa. As a result, acceleration will be at minimum when the velocity is at maximum and vice versa. Therefore, the answer is **D**

12.A Remember that frequency doesn't change when light passes from one phase to another. It always remains constant. As light travels from a denser medium (water) to a rarer medium (air), there is an increase in speed.

The first equation

$$Speed - \lambda \times f$$

As the speed of light increases and frequency remains constant, there is an increase in the wavelength. So, there is an increase in both speed and wavelength. Therefore, the answer is **A**

Important note: As light passes from a denser medium to a rarer medium, there is an increase in speed. Moreover, as light passes from a rarer to denser medium, there is a decrease in speed.

13.B Let's refer to the equation for the harmonics, given the frequency, for a standing wave with two nodes on the edges:

$$f = n\frac{v}{2L}$$

Where n is the number of the harmonic. We don't need to worry about the other variables. The next thing to note is that only the 2nd, 4th, 6th... harmonic actually have a node in the center, so this means that the new n is actually $2n$, which corresponds to answer **B.**

14.C When the resistance of the variable resistor increases, the total resistance of the circuit increases, and this means that the value of current in the circuit will decrease. The voltage of the cell is divided between the two resistors in series depending on the ratio of their resistance (the resistor with a higher resistance has a higher voltage difference). Since the resistance of the variable resistor increases (and the resistance of the other resistor remains constant), the voltmeter connected to the variable resistor will show a higher voltage reading. Therefore, the correct answer is option **C.**

15.C The force in between two plates always acts parallel to them and does not cause any change to the speed of the particle entering. Since the field lines run from positive to negative and we know an electron will be repelled by the negative plate and be attracted to a positive plate (hence it moves in opposite direction of field lines) we can deduce that the answer is **C.**

16.C The combined resistance of the two parallel resistors can be calculated by

$$\frac{1}{R_{total}} = \frac{1}{R_1} + \frac{1}{R_2}$$

Therefore, this is 3 ohms. The total resistance of the circuit is 6 ohms and so the total current travelling through the circuit is 6A if we use $V = IR$ formula. Therefore, the answer is **C.**

17.D Since work done by centripetal force (which acts towards the center of the circle) and the motion of the object (which is tangential to the circle) are perpendicular to each other, there is no work done. This can also be confirmed by using the formula

$$W = Fscos\theta$$

where $\theta = 90°$. So, the answer is **D.**

18.D The actual initial activity of the substance is $240Bq$ when we remove the background radiation. After 36 hours the substance has gone through 4 half-lives which means that the substance has gone through a reduction in activity wherein the resultant activity is given by

$$A = A_0\left(\frac{1}{2^4}\right)$$

Since A_0 was $240Bq$, the final activity after 36 hours is $15Bq$. However, the question does not ask for the activity of the substance, rather it asks for the activity that is recorded (therefore, we must add the background radiation which was given as $20Bq$) to get a final answer of $35Bq$ that is option **D**.

19.A **[Memorize]** An isotope is an atom of the element that has the same number of protons but different number of neutrons. In every alpha-decay, the atom loses 2 neutrons and 2 protons and in every beta-decay the atom loses one neutron and gains one proton. Therefore, if we apply this logic to each of the 4 options we can see that option **A** is correct as the first reaction loses 2 neutrons and 2 protons while the second reaction gains 2 protons and loses 2 neutrons leaving the atom with same number of protons but different number of neutrons. Thus, **A** is the correct answer.

20.B There are no strange particles in this reaction. The lepton number is not conserved because there are 0 leptons on the left side but there is one lepton (the muon) on the right side. Therefore, the answer is **D.**

21.D The power of a wind turbine is given in the data booklet to be

$$P = \frac{1}{2}\rho A v^3$$

By equating the two different scenarios they have mentioned

$$\rho A {v_{ans}}^3 = \frac{\rho A v^3}{2}$$

$$2\rho A {v_{ans}}^3 = \rho A v^3$$

$$2{v_{ans}}^3 = v^3$$

$$v_{ans} = \frac{v}{\sqrt[3]{2}}$$

Therefore, option **D** is the right answer.

22.A The height of each of the power outputs and losses must be measured. We can see that the height of the input energy is 20 units. The energy loss at power station and energy lost to transmission is 15 units. The thermal energy of the lamp is also considered an energy loss because the only useful power output is the light. There are 3 units of energy lost as heat and so the only useful power output is 2 units. This means that the efficiency is

$$Efficiency = \frac{useful\ output\ power}{total\ input\ power} \times 100 = \frac{2}{20} \times 100 = 10\%$$

Therefore, the answer is **A.**

23.A **[Memorize]** The moderator is responsible for slowing down the electrons in a nuclear power station. The slower a neutron travels, the more is the chance for nuclear fission as only a slow neutron can be absorbed my radioactive material for fission to happen. Therefore, option **A** is the right answer.

24.D When resultant force is 0 at a point in time, the object will stop moving. Since the pendulum moves continuously, the force is never 0 and so the answer is **D.**

25.B We know the formula

$$\theta = \frac{\lambda}{b}$$

where θ is the angle from the center to the first dark fringe and λ is the wavelength of the light and b is the slit width. Therefore, reducing the slit width will increase the angle and so the answer is **B.**

26.D The formula for diffraction grating is

$$d = \frac{1}{N}$$

Where N is the number of lines. Moreover, we know that

$$\lambda = \frac{dsin\theta}{n}$$

Since $n = 1$, $\lambda = dsin\theta$. And by replacing the value of d we get

$$\lambda = \frac{sin\theta}{N}$$

The θ in the above equation is simply half of the θ_1 mentioned in the question (because the angle in the question is between both the first order maxima and θ from the formula refers to only half of that angle) and so the formula for wavelength becomes

$$\lambda = \frac{\sin\left(\frac{\theta_1}{2}\right)}{N}$$

Therefore, the answer is **D**.

27.A We know that the speed of sound never changes irrespective of the relative motion between source and observer. For frequency change, since the source is moving towards the observer, we have the formula

$$f' = f\left(\frac{v}{v - u_s}\right)$$

The speed of the train is c/34 while the speed of sound is c, so we have

$$f' = f\left(\frac{c}{c - \frac{c}{34}}\right) = f\left(\frac{c}{\frac{33c}{34}}\right)$$

$$f' = f\left(\frac{34}{33}\right)$$

Since the speed needs to remain the same, since the frequency increases by a ratio of 34/33 the wavelength will have to become 33/34 of what it was initially in order to keep speed same. Therefore, the answer is **A**.

28.C The formula for gravitational potential is

$$V_g = -\frac{GM}{r}$$

If we assume a point A in between the two masses and say that the distance between the planet and point A is y and the distance between the moon and point A is 22R – y we can calculate the sum of their potentials by

$$V_{total} = -GM\left(\frac{100}{y} + \frac{1}{22R - y}\right)$$

Since we need this to be a maximum, let us differentiate it and equate to 0

$$-GM\left(\frac{-100}{y^2} + \frac{1}{(22R - y)^2}\right) = 0$$

Since GM can never be 0

$$\left(\frac{-100}{y^2} + \frac{1}{(22R - y)^2}\right) = 0$$

$$\frac{1}{(22R - y)^2} = \frac{100}{y^2}$$

$$y^2 = 100((22R - y)^2)$$

$$y = 10(22R - y)$$

$$11y = 220R$$

$$y = 20R$$

Therefore, the answer is **C.**

29.A The formula for work done is

$$W = q\Delta V$$

where q is the charge and delta V is the potential difference

When the negative charge moves from its current position to position Y, there is no change in potential (potential remains 100 V). Consequently, the potential difference is 0 and hence according to the formula above, work done is also 0 since work is proportional to potential difference. Now let's consider the case where the negative charge is moved to position X from its current position. It is also important to note that for negative charges, potentials are negative. The charge is quite obviously negative too since it is a negative charge. Now let's use the above formula to compute the work done

$$W = -1 \times (-150V - (-100V))$$
$$= +50nJ$$

Since the charge is in nano coulombs, the work done is in nano joules.

Therefore, the answer is **A.**

Important Note: When negative charge flows from low potential to high potential, the potential difference is negative (since potential values for negative charges are negative). Similarly, when negative charge flows from high potential to low potential, the potential difference is positive.

30.C We know that electric field lines are directed away from positively charged source charges and towards negatively charged charges. Therefore, we can immediately eliminate options A and B since the electric field lines are directed towards the positive point charge, which is incorrect. We also know that electric field lines are always directed perpendicular to the equipotential surfaces and surface of conductors. Clearly option D is incorrect since the electric field lines don't form right angles with the surface of the metal plate. Therefore, the answer is **C.**

31.C Note: This type of question is commonly tested in Physics HL paper 1, hence it is important to acquire a conceptual understanding of the way to approach this type of problem.

The formula for gravitational potential energy is

$$E_p = \frac{-GMm}{R}$$

Similarly, the formula for kinetic energy is

$$E_k = \frac{1}{2}mv^2$$

We know that

$$\frac{mv^2}{R} = \frac{GM}{R^2}$$

since centripetal force equals the gravitational force

Note: centripetal force is not a fundamental force but a net force that acts on an object. In this case, the centripetal force equals the gravitational force. In the case where a car moves in a circular track, the centripetal force is nothing but the force of friction.

Thus, we can deduce that

$$E_k = \frac{1}{2} \times \frac{GM}{R}$$

From the question we know that the satellite moves from orbit X to Y. Orbit Y is clearly farther away from the planet than Orbit X. Therefore, the value of R (Distance between the center of the planet and the satellite) increases. An increase in R causes the potential energy to become less negative (we can deduce this from the formula of potential energy derived above). Therefore, there is an increase in the gravitational potential energy. Similarly, an increase in R leads to decrease in the positivity of the kinetic energy. Therefore, the kinetic energy decreases.

Therefore, the answer is **C**.

32.C From the formula booklet, we know that

$$V_{esc} = \sqrt{\frac{2GM}{R}}$$

Escape speed from the earth

$$V_{earth} = \sqrt{\frac{2GM_E}{R_E}}$$

Escape speed from the moon

$$V_{moon} = \sqrt{\frac{2GM_M}{R_M}}$$

Ratio of the two escape speeds

$$= \sqrt{\frac{2GM_E}{R_E}} \div \sqrt{\frac{2GM_M}{R_M}}$$

$$= \sqrt{\frac{M_E R_M}{M_M R_E}}$$

Therefore, the answer is **C.**

33.C This question is related to Lenz's law. Lenz law states that an induced electric current flow in a direction such that the current opposes the change that induced it. From the very first line of the question, we know that the current flowing in loop A is increasing. As a result, the magnetic field is increasing everywhere. Therefore, according to Lenz law, induced current in B and C must such that it causes a decrease in magnetic field. Using right hand grip rule, we can deduce that the current should be anti-clockwise at B and clockwise at C. Therefore, the correct answer is option **C.**

34.A Faraday's law states that induced emf is equal to the rate of change of total flux linkage (essentially the rate of change of magnetic field passing through).

As the flat coil begins to enter the magnetic field, there is a rate of change (from no magnetic field to some). However, once the coil is entirely the field because the field is uniform, there is no longer any change, so induced emf is 0 at the middle part.

Once the coil emerges, there is a change of magnetic field (from some to none), but in the opposite charge as the coil is moving in the opposite direction relative to the normal of the magnetic field.

The only option which shows initial emf, no emf and then some emf in the negative direction is **A.**

35.A From the formula booklet, we know that

$$P_{avg} = \frac{V_{rms}^{\ 2}}{R}$$

$$= \frac{60^2}{100}$$

$$= 36W$$

From the graph given in the question, we can deduce that,

$$Time\ period, T = \ 2 \times 0.02 = 0.04s$$

Next, we need to calculate the frequency of the ac power supply,

$$Frequency = \frac{1}{Time\ Period}$$

$$= \frac{1}{0.04}$$

$$= 25\ Hz$$

Therefore, the answer is **A.**

36.C Let's calculate the combined capacitance of the given circuits in each of the options.

Option A.

$$\frac{1}{C_t} = \frac{1}{C} + \frac{1}{C} + \frac{1}{C} = \frac{3}{C}$$

$$C_t = \frac{C}{3}$$

Option B.

$$C_t = C + C + C = 3C$$

For option C we have a series Arrangement,

$$\frac{1}{C_{series}} = \frac{1}{C} + \frac{1}{C} = \frac{2}{C}$$

$$C_{series} = \frac{C}{2}$$

Complete Capacitance,

$$C_t = \frac{C}{2} + C = 1.5C$$

Therefore, the answer is **C.**

37.A From the formula booklet, we can deduce the formula for maximum kinetic energy of electrons that leave the cathode,

$$E_{max} = hf - \phi$$

$$= 6eV - 3eV = 3eV$$

Stopping potential decreases the kinetic energy by,

$$qV = 2eV$$

Thus, maximum kinetic energy of electrons reaching the anode,

$$3\ eV - 2\ eV = 1\ eV$$

Therefore, the answer is **A.**

38.B We know that diffraction is a property of waves and therefore, electron diffraction from crystals is an evidence for the wave nature of the electron. Therefore, the answer is **B.**

39.B Tunneling is a phenomenon that occurs due to a temporary uncertainty in energy. It is important to remember that an electron will not lose any energy after tunneling due to conservation of energy. Therefore, the energy will remain constant and the answer is **B.**

40.C The question is a little ambiguous. What it really means is that both samples initially had the same activity, but <u>after a fixed amount of time,</u> sample X has half the particles (and therefore, half the activity) of sample Y. This implies that, that in this fixed time, sample Y has undergone <u>one more</u> halving of its activity than sample X.

The simplest way this could have happened is that, in the time, sample X underwent one half-life and sample Y underwent two. This would mean the half-life of Y is half that of X, which is found in option **C**.

1.D We know that

$$Density\ (\rho) = \frac{mass\ (m)}{volume\ (V)}$$

Let's find the fractional uncertainty of density

$$\frac{\Delta\rho}{\rho} = \frac{\Delta m}{m} + \frac{\Delta V}{V}$$

We know that $Volume\ (V) = Length^3$. Now let's find the fractional uncertainty of volume

$$\frac{\Delta V}{V} = 3 \times \frac{\Delta L}{L}$$

Percentage uncertainty of the volume of the cube $\left(\frac{\Delta V}{V} \times 100\right) = 3 \times \frac{\Delta L}{L} \times 100$

$$= 3 \times 4 = 12\%$$

Percentage uncertainty of the mass of the cube $= 8\%$ (given in the question)

Percentage uncertainty of the density of the cube

$$\left(\frac{\Delta\rho}{\rho} \times 100\right) = \frac{\Delta m}{m} \times 100\ (\%\ uncertainty\ of\ mass) + \frac{\Delta V}{V} \times 100\ (\%\ uncertainty\ of\ volume)$$

$$= 8 + 12 = 20\%$$

Therefore, the answer is D

2.C We know that

$$v^2 = u^2 + 2as$$

The question tells us that the initial speed is $20\ ms^{-1}$ and deceleration is $4.0\ ms^{-2}$

Since the truck comes to stop, the final velocity (v) $= 0$

$0^2 = 20^2 - 2 \times 4 \times s$ (acceleration is negative since the object is decelerating)

$$s = \frac{-400}{-8} = 50\ m$$

Therefore, the answer is **C**

3.A We know that

$$v^2 = u^2 + 2as$$

Since the runner starts from rest, initial velocity (u) = 0

$$v^2 = 2as$$

$$v = \sqrt{2as}$$

Notice that the x-axis of the graph is distance travelled and not time, so do read the question carefully. Hence, the equation of the graph is

$$v = \sqrt{2as}$$

By looking at the shape of the graph, it is possible to deduce the form of the graph equation

Option A: Graph equation will have the form $y = \sqrt{x}$

Option B: Graph equation will have the form $y = x$

Option C: Graph equation will have the form $y = c, where\ c\ is\ a\ constant$

Option D: Graph equation will have the form $y = x^2$

Option A is the only graph that corresponds with the equation

$$v = \sqrt{2as}$$

Therefore, the answer is **A**

Important note: Mathematical knowledge is an integral part of solving physics paper 1 questions and sometimes you will be forced to apply what you learnt in Math HL/SL in physics problems

---

4.A When the projectile falls from O towards the ground, the projectile accelerates. Since the projectile accelerates, there is an increase in the magnitude of the vertical component of the velocity (Remember that acceleration is the increase in velocity per unit time). Notice that the graph given is asymmetric (which is unconventional!).

This tells us that air resistance is present. The graph will only be symmetric if air resistance is negligible (during projectile motion, the only force that acts is the force of gravity). As a result, the projectile moves less horizontal distance after reaching the peak (quite apparent from the graph). So, this means that the horizontal component of velocity decreases and thus, the correct answer is option **A**.

5.A The tension in the string at the top of the circle acts downwards. When the mass is at the top of the circle, the weight of the mass acts downwards.

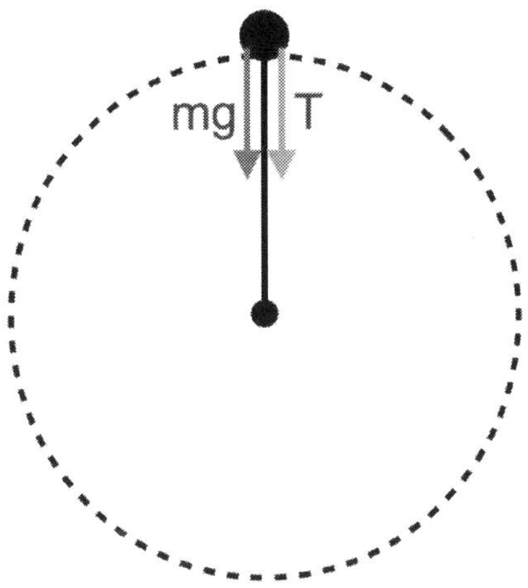

We know that the resultant force is centripetal force (F) that acts towards the center of the circle. In this question, the resultant force is weight + tension (T) since both forces act towards the center of the circle

$$F = \frac{mv^2}{R}$$

$$\frac{mv^2}{R} = mg + T$$

$$mv^2 = R(mg + T)$$

We know that Kinetic energy $= \frac{1}{2}mv^2$

$$\frac{1}{2}mv^2 = \frac{R(mg + T)}{2}$$

Therefore, the answer is **A.**

6.B We know that

$$v = \omega x_0 cos(\omega t)$$

where x_0 is the distance through which the spring is compressed (aka amplitude)
From the equation, it is clear that velocity is directly proportional to the amplitude
When the speed of the object halves, x_0 will also halve according to the first equation
Therefore, the answer is **B.**

7.B For this question, we need to calculate the resultant force of F_1 and F_2 which is done by drawing a parallelogram for all the options as shown in the diagram below:

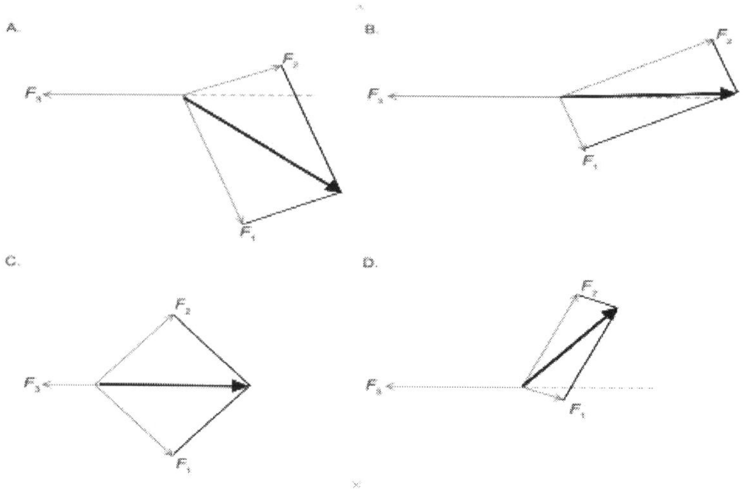

The resultant force is the diagonal of this parallelogram and we can clearly see that it looks equal in magnitude to F_3 and acts in the opposite direction, thus balancing the forces acting on the object. Therefore, the correct answer is option **B.**

8.C Note that the solid substance has just reached its melting point, which means that it is melting (solid to liquid). During melting, the temperature is constant since the energy supplied is used to break the bonds in the solid molecules and increase the inter-particle potential energy. This energy doesn't raise the kinetic energy of the substance, so there is no change in temperature. Once the melting process is complete and all the solid is converted into liquid, the energy supplied is used to raise the kinetic energy of the liquid molecules, which causes rise in temperature. The energy supplied doesn't increase the inter-particle potential energy anymore since there is no more phase change. The graph in option C corresponds with these deductions. Therefore, the answer is **C**

Important note: There is no temperature change during any phase change (melting, boiling, freezing, condensing and so on) since the energy supplied alters the potential energy of the particles in the substance rather than changing the average kinetic energy of the molecules in the substance.

9.C We know that

$$\overline{E_k} = \frac{1}{2}mv^2$$

$$v = \sqrt{\frac{2\overline{E_k}}{m}}$$

Since the container is filled with a mixture of helium and oxygen at the same temperature, the average kinetic energy of helium and oxygen is the same. Remember that average kinetic energy is directly proportional to the temperature. Same temperature implies same average kinetic energy.

Now let us find the ratio asked in the question

$$= \frac{\sqrt{\frac{2\overline{E_k}}{m_{helium}}}}{\sqrt{\frac{2\overline{E_k}}{m_{oxygen}}}}$$

$$= \sqrt{\frac{m_{oxygen}}{m_{helium}}}$$

$$= \sqrt{\frac{32}{4}}$$

$$= \sqrt{8}$$

Therefore, the answer is **C.**

10.C We know the formula

$$pV = nRT$$

and so $T = \frac{pV}{nR}$. Since R is the same for both X and Y, the only quantities that affect the ratio are pressure, volume, and moles. Let $2p$ be the pressure of X, V be the volume of X and n be the number of moles of X, then the ratio:

$$\frac{T_X}{T_Y} = \frac{\frac{2pV}{n}}{\frac{p4V}{2n}} = \frac{2pV}{n} \times \frac{2n}{p4V} = 1$$

Therefore, the correct answer is option **C.**

11.B Frequency is defined as the number of oscillations or occurrences of a repeating event per unit time. We know that 5 revolutions take 3 seconds.

$$3\ seconds = 5\ revolutions$$

$$1\ second = \frac{5 \times 1}{3} revolutions$$

Therefore, the answer is **B**

12.B **[Memorize]** In a transverse wave, the particles of the medium move perpendicular to the direction of the propagation of the wave (which is also the direction of energy transfer). In a longitudinal wave, the particles of the medium move parallel to it. The direction of energy transfer is the same as the direction of the propagation of wave always. Therefore, the correct answer is option **B.**

13.A We know that intensity is inversely proportional to the distance

$$\left(I \propto \frac{1}{x^2}\right)$$

The intensity of the light at a distance $2x$ from L is I

$$I \propto \frac{1}{(2x)^2} = \frac{k}{4x^2}$$

The intensity of light at a distance $3x$ from L is I_{3x}

$$I_{3x} = \frac{k}{(3x)^2} = \frac{k}{9x^2} = \frac{4}{9} \times \frac{k}{4x^2} = \frac{4}{9}I$$

Therefore, the answer is **A**

14.D Let's assume that the amplitude of waves from coherent sources X and Y is A. Waves from X and Y will eventually superpose each other. The path difference of the waves is $6 - 5.6 = 0.4\,m$. This path difference is an integral multiple of the wavelength (path difference $= 2\lambda$ since $\lambda = 0.2\,m$). Since path difference is in the form $n\lambda$ rather than

$$\left(n + \frac{1}{2}\right)\lambda$$

(where n is an integer), constructive interference takes places (in other words, the maxima of the two waves add together).

According to the principle of superposition, the resultant displacement of the superposed wave is the vector sum of the individual displacements of the two respective waves. Hence, the amplitude of the new superposed wave is A + A = 2A

We know that the intensity of the wave is proportional to the square of the amplitude, so $I = kA^2$, where k is a constant. The resultant wave has an amplitude 2A, so

$$I_{new} = k(2A)^2 = 4kA^2 = 4I$$

Therefore, the answer is **D**

15.A Since the angle of incidence of the light is greater than the critical angle, light will undergo total internal reflection (complete reflection of a ray of light).
Important note: For total internal reflection to take place, light needs to travel from a denser medium to a rarer medium. Light travelling from a rarer to denser medium cannot undergo total internal reflection. This rules out option C and D. Also note that during total internal reflection, light is reflected back to the same medium and there is NO refracted ray. This rules out option B. Therefore, the answer is **A**.

16.B We know that

$$R = \frac{\rho L}{A}$$

As the length doubles, the resistance also doubles according to the above equation
We also know that

$$Power = \frac{V^2}{R}$$

When wire of length L is used, the power dissipated is 1000 W. When wire of length $2L$ is used, resistance will double. Since the potential difference stays the same (stated in the question), the power will halve according to the second equation. Therefore, the answer is **B** (500 W)

17.C Firstly, let us find the resistance of the entire circuit. We'll start by calculating the resistance of the parallel arrangement in the circuit ($R_{parallel}$). Remember that all the resistors are identical.

$$\frac{1}{2R} + \frac{1}{R} = \frac{1}{R_{parallel}}$$

$$R_{parallel} = \frac{2R}{3}$$

Next, we'll find the total resistance of the circuit by calculating resistance of the series arrangement in the circuit

$$R_{total} = \frac{2R}{3} + R = \frac{5R}{3}$$

Next, we'll find out the total current passing through the circuit

$$I = \frac{V}{R} = \frac{\varepsilon}{\left(\frac{5R}{3}\right)} = \frac{3\varepsilon}{5R}$$

This current is NOT the current that passes through the resistor X.

Now let us calculate the voltage across X (which is total voltage - voltage across the single resistor). Voltage is same across each component of the parallel circuit

$$V_X = \varepsilon - IR$$

$$V_X = \varepsilon - \frac{3\varepsilon}{5} = \frac{2\varepsilon}{5}$$

Now that we know the voltage across X and the resistance of X, we can finally calculate the current passing through it

$$I_X = \frac{V_X}{R_X} = \frac{\left(\frac{2\varepsilon}{5}\right)}{R} = \frac{2\varepsilon}{5R}$$

Therefore, the answer is **C**

18.A For the arrow from S to point downwards, we need the magnetic field direction of P to be clockwise and the field direction of Q to be anti-clockwise so that they add up in the downward direction. For P to have a clockwise magnetic field, it needs to have current going into the page (which can be found out using right hand rule). For Q to have an anti-clockwise magnetic field direction, it needs to have current going out of the page. Therefore, the correct answer is option **A**.

19.B The force acting on the particle due to the field is given by the formula $F = Bqvsin\theta$ and since $\theta = 90°$, $F = Bqv$. This force provides the centripetal force for the particle and so we can equate

$$\frac{mv^2}{R} = Bqv$$

And so,

$$v = \frac{qBR}{m}$$

To find the charge of the particle, we need to use Fleming's left-hand rule. Let your pointer finger point into the page, and your thumb point downwards, then you can see that the conventional current direction (indicated by your middle finger) is leftwards. This means that the particle moving is in the opposite charge of the conventional current flow and this means that the particle is negative. Therefore, the correct answer is option **B.**

20.B Neutrons have neutral charge and as a result, will not affect the scattering of alpha particles. Therefore, II is not true. The deflection was due to the electric force of repulsion between the positive charge of the atom and the positive charge of alpha particle, so I is true. The large deflection can be explained by the alpha particle's interaction with the small and concentrated nucleus that is positively charged. By measuring the percentage of particles deflected through large particles, Rutherford was able to come up with the conclusion that the radius of the nucleus is much smaller than the radius of the atom. Therefore, the answer is **B.**

Useful tip: Close reading of nuclear and quantum physics chapter is essential for answering such questions since the questions asked from these topics are very intricate and probe into minor details mentioned in the chapter. Therefore, you must read the chapter thoroughly. Prior knowledge of the Rutherford experiment is essential for solving this question with ease.

---

21. A Iterating through the three statements:

I. In the latter half of the graph, the line tends upwards away from the 45° diagonal, so at high z **I can** be inferred

II. In the first half of the graph, the line is exactly 45°. As the scales are even, that means N=Z in this range, so **II can** be inferred

III. Atomic number of a nucleus is the same as the number of protons. As shown in II, the number of neutrons is equal to protons for small Z, so **III cannot** be true

This combination is option **A.**

22. B We can solve this problem just by thinking about the lepton number. In the left half of the equation, μ^- (the muon) has a lepton number of 1. However, both e^- (the electron) and v_μ (the muon neutrino) have lepton numbers of 1. Therefore, to balance the equation, we must choose for X a particle with a lepton number of (-1). The only option that fulfills this criterion is $\bar{v}_e$, the electron antineutrino, option **B.**

---

23. D **[Memorize]** Control rods stop unstable nuclei from escaping its bounds. They can therefore be used to regulate the rate of a nuclear reaction by stopping the reaction from growing. Therefore, the correct answer is option **D.**

---

24. D The different efficiencies of the photovoltaic panel implies the following:

> If they are the same surface area, the second panel will produce 15 units of power for every 20 units of power the first panel produces.

Given that surface area is proportional to total power produced, surface area for the second panel must increase by the same fractional amount that efficiency is reduced to make them produce the same power. Therefore, the new area will be

$$\left(\frac{15}{20}\right)^{-1} S = \frac{4}{3} S$$

This corresponds to option **D.**

---

25. B The light ray is reflected off the snow-covered Earth and then reflected off the cloud. As the reflections happen in succession, we must multiply each albedo:

$$I_0 \times 0.80 \times 0.30 = 0.24 I_0$$

This corresponds to option **B.**

---

26. C The time-period for an SHM oscillation is not affected by its amplitude*. On the other hand, as per section 9.1 of the data booklet:

$$E_T = \frac{1}{2}\omega^2 x_0^2$$

The energy of the oscillation is proportional to amplitude, x_0, squared, so halving amplitude will reduce total energy by a factor of 4. This combination is found in option **C.**

*At low oscillation angles, which we can assume is the case for all IB SHM questions

27. C Iterating through the three statements:

I. As slits increase, the makeup of each primary maxima will change, but not the separation between them. Note that in the diagram given all the curves make up only one primary maxima. Therefore, increasing slits **does not** change this.

II. As the number of slits increases, energy is more focused, so the maximum intensity of the primary maxima **does** increase

III. As the number of slits increase, each primary maxima **does** become narrower (recall that using a diffraction grating, a very large number of slits, makes the maxima so narrow they appear as straight lines)

This combination is found in **C**

---

28. B As per section 9.3 of the data booklet,

$$n\lambda = d \sin\theta$$

Rearranging to isolate the wavelength:

$$\lambda = \frac{d\sin\theta}{n}$$

Recall that n is the order of maxima, while θ is its angle from the zero order. The only order for which we know the angle with certainty is $n = 2$ for which the angle is β. Substituting that into the rearranged equation returns expression **B.**

---

29. D Because the ambulance is moving and the observer is stationary, we use the equation for 'moving source' from section 9.5 of the data booklet:

$$f^{\prime} = f\left(\frac{v}{v \pm u_s}\right)$$

Here, v is the speed of sound in air and u_s is the relative speed between the source and observer. Because the source is moving towards the observer, the sound waves are compressed even more by the moving source, so frequency is greater, and we subtract u_s. Substituting our known values gives the expression:

$$1200 \times \left(\frac{330}{330 - 40}\right) = \frac{1200 \times 330}{290} \text{Hz}$$

Which corresponds to answer **D**.

30. D There isn't much information given in this question. However, we do know that when $x = 0.8$, the graph is at a minimum point, so its gradient is 0. As it stands, the gradient, or rate of change of, voltage as distance varies is also known as gravitational field strength. Now we're getting somewhere! Therefore, the correct answer is option **D.**

---

31. A **[Memorize]** The definition of gravitational potential is:
Work done per unit mass to move a point mass from infinity to P
Therefore, the correct answer is option **A.**

---

32. D As per section 10.2 of the data booklet, the escape velocity v_{esc} for a given body is:

$$v_{esc} = \sqrt{\frac{2GM}{r}}$$

Let's determine how M, the mass of the planet, and r, its radius, changes. The latter of these is straightforward; r becomes $2r$ for the new planet. What about M? We know that density of Planet X is half that of Earth. The equation for density is:

$$\rho = \frac{Mass}{Volume}$$

Rearranging to isolate Mass, we get:

$$Mass = \rho \times Volume$$

For the new planet, ρ is halved, and, because radius is twice as large, we know that volume increases by a factor of 2^3. Therefore, the new mass is $2^3 \div 2 = 4$ times greater. Substituting this into the equation, and then substituting v_{esc}:

$$v_{\text{Planet x}} = \sqrt{\frac{2G(4M)}{(2r)}} = \sqrt{\frac{4}{2}} \times \sqrt{\frac{2GM}{r}} = \sqrt{\frac{4}{2}} \times v_{esc}$$

This is $\sqrt{2}v_{esc}$, option **D.**

---

33. D Faraday's law states that:

$$\text{Emf} = N\frac{\Delta BA}{\Delta T}$$

Where B is the external magnetic field, A is the area, T is the time taken and N is the number of turns. For a 180° turn, N is 1 but ΔB varies from +X to -X, so the change in B is 2X. Area and time are unchanged from the question, so the net result is that

$$Emf = \frac{2XS}{T}$$

Which corresponds to option **D.**

---

34. C When frequency is decreased, the time period of oscillation increases. This narrows down our options to C and D, the two graphs for which the intervals on the x axis go up by two rather than one. In addition, as per Faraday's law, induced EMF is given by the equation:

$$\text{Emf} = N\frac{\Delta BA}{\Delta T}$$

This means that Emf is proportional to the number of rotations, N, in a given time period:

$$Emf \propto \frac{N}{\Delta T}$$

This expression can be taken to mean frequency. As a result, as frequency reduces, so does maximum power. This narrows down the choice to option **C**.

35. A The question states that the setup is a step-up transformer. This means that the output voltage will be higher than the input voltage. The equation for the ratio of primary to secondary voltage (V_p and V_s) is:

$$\frac{N_p}{N_s} = \frac{V_p}{V_s}$$

As V_s for a step-up transformer will be greater than V_p, we know that N_s must be higher than N_p. Given that the question states that one coil has 1000 times as many turns, we know the ratio of turns is:

$$\frac{N_p}{N_s} = \frac{1}{1000}$$

This narrows down our choice to options A and C. In an ideal transformer, input power is equal to output power. As power is equal to current multiplied by voltage, we can generate the following equation with primary and secondary current (I_p and I_s):

$$V_p I_p = V_s I_s$$

And therefore that:

$$\frac{I_s}{I_p} = \frac{V_p}{V_s} = \frac{N_p}{N_s} = \frac{1}{1000}$$

This tells us that the current in the secondary coil is the primary current divided by 1000, which corresponds to option **A**.

36. C The given diagram can be redrawn with no loss of accuracy as the following:

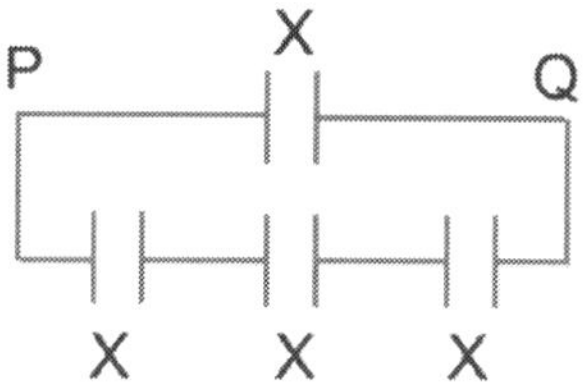

Now it is clear that there are two paths in parallel – one made of a singular capacitor and another made of three capacitors in series, all with capacitance X. Given the equations for capacitance in series and parallel:

$$C = X + \left(\frac{1}{X} + \frac{1}{X} + \frac{1}{X}\right)^{-1}$$

$$X + \left(\frac{3}{X}\right)^{-1}$$

$$X + \frac{X}{3} = \frac{4X}{3}$$

This corresponds to option **C.**

37. C If no photoelectrons are emitted in such an experiment, there are only two ways to make them:

1. Using a metal plate with a smaller work function
2. Increasing the frequency of radiation

This second option is found in option **C**, as reducing wavelength increases frequency for light, which has constant wave speed.

---

38. D Let's first consider the two actions – 'pair annihilation' and 'pair production'. Pair annihilation occurs when a particle meets its antiparticle and leads to the two particles annihilating each other to form 2 photons. Because no diagram shows photons, we know that, in this case, the two photons immediately undergo 'pair production'. Here, the photons produce another pair of particles.
That's the context, but how do we narrow down our choice of diagrams? We can take a shortcut here – by observing the rule that at any given vertex on a Feynman Diagram, only one particle can point in and only one can point out. For diagrams A and C, the left e^+ and e^- point inwards, so we eliminate those. On diagram B, both e^+ and e^- point outwards on the right. This leaves **D.**

---

39. D From section 12.2 of the data booklet, we know that the relationship between activity, A, the decay constant λ, time t and initial number of nuclei N_0:

$$A = -\lambda N_0 e^{-\lambda t}$$

The graph plots ln(activity) so let's take the natural logarithm of both sides:

$$lnA = ln(\lambda N_0\} - \lambda t$$

This can be interpreted as a straight-line graph in the form $y = mt + c$ where m is $-\lambda$ and c is $ln(\lambda N_0)$. We don't need to worry about the unknown N_0 term in c because we can use the gradient of the graph in the question to work out λ directly. The gradient of the graph is -6, making λ equal 6, **D**.

---

40. A Iterating through the three options:

I. The activity of the nuclide **is** needed so it can be compared to the theoretical past activity

II. The number of nuclide atoms **is** needed to compare to the theoretical starting number of nuclide atoms

III. The mass number does not change regardless of the half-life of the nuclide, so is **not** relevant

This combination is option **A.**

May 2019 TZ1

1.B The formula for calculating percentage uncertainty is

$$\left(\frac{\Delta\lambda}{\lambda}+\frac{\Delta Y}{Y}+\frac{\Delta z}{z}\right)*100$$

But since the values given are already in terms of percentage, we must add them up to get 15.05% and so the answer is **B.**

2.A The equation is

$$p = x + yT$$

In terms of units we have

$$Pa = ? + ?\cdot K$$

Since $Pressure = Force/Area$, the unit of Pascals can be written as

$$\frac{N}{m^2} = \frac{kgm/s^2}{m^2} = kg/ms^2$$

And so

$$\frac{kg}{ms^2} = ? + ?\cdot K$$

Since there is no K on the LHS, we know that the unit of y must have a K^{-1} so that K gets cancelled. Moreover, we need kg/ms^2 on the LHS so this becomes the unit of x in the RHS. This is essentially $kgm^{-1}s^{-2}$. However, we cannot add two things with different units and so there must be $kgm^{-1}s^{-2}$ in the unit of Y so that it can be added with x. Therefore, the unit of Y will become $kgm^{-1}s^{-2}K^{-1}$ and so the answer is **A.**

3.C When she opens her parachute, she is still moving downwards, so the direction of the velocity vector is downwards. However, when the parachute is open, the magnitude of air resistance is much more than the weight acting towards and so the net force (and thus acceleration) is in an upward direction. Therefore, the answer is **C.**

4.C Let us calculate the speed in m/s so we get 100000m/hour and so the change per second is $\frac{100000}{60*60} = 27.77$

And so, the acceleration is

$$\frac{\Delta v}{\Delta t} = \frac{27.77}{3} = 9.26m/s^2$$

In terms of g, this is closest to 0.9g since $g = 9.81ms^{-2}$ and the answer is **C.**

5.D Since it travels x meters in 0.5s, the initial velocity of the object is 2m/s. The object falls downwards with a constant acceleration that equals g. We can calculate displacement as we know it falls y meters in first 0.5 seconds and so with an acceleration of 9.81m/s^2 we know that it has gone $9.81/4$ meters in first 0.5 seconds and will reach 9.81 meters at the end of first second and so it travels a distance that is 4 times greater. Therefore, the answer is **D**.

6.A Since the velocity does not change, we know that there is no change in kinetic energy. This means that all the change in potential energy has been transformed to thermal energy. Since the object moves down a height h, the change in GPE can be calculated by mgh. Therefore, the answer is **A**.

7.D There are only two forces acting on the tray. One is the weight of the tray which acts directly downwards, and the other is normal reaction whose direction is decided by the way the tray is being held. Since the tray is tilted slightly, the normal reaction force direction is also tilted slightly to the right. But since it is accelerating in a rightward direction, the normal reaction force must be greater than the weight and therefore, we can deduce that **D** is the right answer.

8.D The temperature remains the same as there is no temperature change during changes of state (such as melting and boiling). The rate of vaporization increases because there is more thermal energy provided which is used to change more of water into vapour form. Thus, the answer is **D**.

9.B We know the formula

$$Q = Mc\Delta T$$

And in this case the total mass (M) will be nm. Let us calculate the energy gained by the particles because of the loss in potential energy using the formula

$$Q = mgh = mgL$$

And since, there are n particles, and they are inverted s times, the total energy will be

$$Q = snmgL$$

Now, if we equate the two formulae, we will get

$$nmc\Delta T = snmgL$$

$$c = \frac{sgL}{\Delta T}$$

Therefore, the correct answer is option **B**.

10.C We know the formula

$$PV = nRT$$

And also

$$PV = \frac{N}{N_A}RT$$

Since R and V remained the same, we only need to worry about N and T. We know that

$$\frac{P1}{P2} = \frac{N1T1}{N2T2}$$

$$\frac{20}{P2} = \frac{\frac{NT}{6TN}}{4}$$

$$\frac{120}{4} = P2$$

Therefore, we know that the answer is **B.**

11.C We know that displacement is in the form of a sine curve and acceleration is in the form of a negative sine curve (as we get $-\sin(x)$ when you differentiate $\sin(x)$ twice. Therefore, the phase difference between these two graphs is π and so the answer is **C.**

12.D We know two things about kinetic energy in SHM. It is always positive, and it goes from 0 to maximum to 0. Within one oscillation, the kinetic energy reaches a maximum value twice (once while going away from starting point and one while coming back to the starting point). Therefore, this answer is **D.**

13.D This question asks for a situation of total internal reflection and so option **D** is the only graph that makes sense.

14.B At first, we have a pipe with one closed end at the node. At this point the distance between node and antinode, x, is equal to ¼ of the wavelength. Therefore,

$$\lambda = 4x$$

In the second case, the distance between the two nodes is y and so that distance is equal to ½ of the wavelength + ½ of the wavelength so in essence it is ¾ of the wavelength. So we have

$$\frac{3}{4}\lambda = y$$

So,

$$\lambda = \frac{4}{3}y$$

Therefore, the answer will be **B**.

15.D Since the two direction of charges are opposite and they are of opposite charge it essentially means there is 0.2C of charge flowing through the circuit. Current is the amount of charge flowing per second and so there is 0.2A in the circuit which leads us to option **D**.

16.A We know that

$$W = VQ$$

If V is changed to V/2, the work done also reduces to W/2. The increase in distance between the plates does not affect the kinetic energy. Therefore, the answer is **A**.

17.B Since there are 2 identical resistors which equally share the dissipated power, they each must get

$$\frac{Pt}{2}$$

amount of energy and so out of all the options only option **B** is able to give that much amount of energy.

18.A We should first find the direction of the magnetic field using right hand grip rule. Then you must apply Fleming's Left-hand rule to find out the direction of the thrust. For the wire on the left, this will be acting rightwards and for the wire on the right, it is acting leftwards. Therefore, option **A** is the right option.

19.B Using Fleming's LHR, we get the force to be acting in the direction of option **B**, as the magnetic field is in the direction of south-east and the current is directed towards us from out of the page.

20.D From

$$F = ma$$

We know

$$a = \frac{F}{m}$$

And for gravitational force we know it can be calculated by

$$F = \frac{GMm}{r^2}$$

Therefore,

$$a = \frac{GM}{r^2}$$

Since the radius of satellite Y orbit is 2 times bigger, the acceleration of satellite Y will be ¼ of the acceleration of satellite X. Therefore, the ratio asked in the question is the one shown in option **D**.

21.A If we need to travel at a greater speed, we need more friction to enable us to do that. We also need a greater proportion of the motorcyclist's normal reaction acting towards the centre of the circle. Therefore, theoretically it makes sense to make the motorcyclist tilt more towards the circle and increasing the coefficient of friction will mean more centripetal force is provided to the motorcyclist. Therefore, option **A** is correct.

22.A Notice that the top diagram is going left to right with increasing wavelength. This means that low energy transitions are on the right. There are two such low energy transitions (represented by the two lines on the right). This means that our solution must have two sets of energy levels that are close together. Only A and D have this. From here, we can use the process of elimination; specifically, if D were correct, there would be two transitions with about half the energy of the maximum transition but there are no such lines in the top diagram. Therefore, option D cannot be the right answer. This means that option **A** is the correct answer.

23.B This has to be beta-minus decay as only then will the atomic numbers be balanced on both sides. Moreover, in beta-minus decay an electron antineutrino is always released so the answer is **B**.

24.B We must calculate the initial energy of the atom and the final energy of the atom using

$$E = mc^2$$

Initially, the total energy was mc^2.
After splitting the energy is calculated by

$$(2m_p + m_n)c^2$$

If we calculate the difference between the two and divide by the number of nucleons, we get

$$\frac{(2m_p + m_n - m)c^2}{3}$$

Therefore, option **B** is the right answer.

25.B **[Memorize]** Solar energy only relies on the sun's heat to create electrical energy. Therefore, option B is the correct answer.

26.C We know

$$Q = mc\Delta T$$

Dividing both sides by change in time we get

$$P = mc\left(\frac{\Delta T}{\Delta t}\right)$$

Therefore

$$\frac{P}{mc} = \frac{\Delta T}{\Delta t}$$

$$\frac{400}{4200} = \frac{\Delta T}{\Delta t}$$

So, the correct answer is **C**.

27.D Simply, this situation only closely mirrors the phenomena of refraction and so the answer is **D.** However, it may be useful to know Fermat's last theorem which states that the path taken by light to move between point A to point B is always the path of shortest distance. And so when it goes from one medium to another it is bound to undergo refraction.

28.D Option **D** has the highest centre of mass and so the least length of the pendulum. Since the formula for time period is

$$T = 2\pi\sqrt{\frac{l}{g}}$$

And so it will have the shortest period. Thus, the correct answer is option **D.**

29.C We know that

$$s = \frac{\lambda D}{d}$$

And therefore, only option **C** works as we are increasing D (the distance from slit to screen).

30.B We know the angle can be found using

$$\theta = \frac{\lambda}{b}$$

And so

$$\theta = 1.22\left(\frac{400 \times 10^{-9}}{4.0 \times 10^{-3}}\right)$$

We can now use the trigonometric relationship to get

$$1.22\frac{400 \times 10^{-9}}{4.0 \times 10^{-3}} = \frac{1.2}{X}$$

So X is roughly 10000m which is 10km. Therefore, the correct answer is option **B.**

31.D When light from a rarer medium hits a denser medium, it undergoes a phase change of π. Since we know the formula for destructive interference happening in thin film is

$$2nx = \frac{\lambda}{2}$$

Where n is refractive index and x is the thickness of the film. Therefore we have

$$3x = \frac{\lambda}{2}$$

$$x = \frac{\lambda}{6}$$

Therefore, the answer is **D**.

32.D As field lines move from positive to negative, the direction of option **D** means that the negative charge needs to overcome the repulsion of the negative charge and the attraction of the positive side which pulls it leftward and so the charge needs to do the greatest amount of work in order to overcome those forces.

33.C The formula for escape speed is

$$V_{esc} = \sqrt{\frac{2GM}{R}}$$

By subbing in values for the moon

$$V_{esc} = \sqrt{\frac{\frac{2GM}{81}}{\frac{R}{4}}}$$

$$V_{esc} = \sqrt{\frac{8GM}{81R}}$$

$$V_{esc} = \frac{2}{9}\sqrt{\frac{2GM}{R}}$$

Therefore, the answer is **C**.

34.C From the data booklet formula, we can see that the orbital velocity

$$\left(v = \sqrt{\frac{GM}{R}}\right)$$

is inversely proportional to the radius. So as radius reduces, the orbital velocity increases and so kinetic energy increases. Always when moving in the direction of the gravitational force means that the object does negative work (and does positive work when moving against gravity). Therefore, since the object is moving in the same direction as the gravitational force, the work done is negative. So, the answer is **C.**

35.B The gradient of the magnetic flux graph gives the magnitude of the induced emf which can be concluded from

$$\varepsilon = -\frac{N\Delta\Phi}{\Delta t}$$

Therefore, the answer is **B** which has all the points where the gradient is highest.

36.A The total capacitance of the circuit can be found by

$$\frac{1}{C} = \frac{1}{C_1} + \frac{1}{C_2}$$

Therefore, this adds up to 2 ($C = 2$). Charge on plates can be found by using the formula

$$Q = CV$$

And so the charge is 18, so the answer is **A** as both capacitors are connected in series.

37.C Since this is a discharge process, the current has to be decreasing. Moreover, the amount of current can be found by using

$$I = \frac{V}{R}$$

And so the answer is **C.**

38.A Ultraviolet light has a greater frequency than infra-red and since

$$E = hf - \phi$$

The photoelectrons have more energy and thus more kinetic energy. The same intensity means that there should be same energy per second and so it takes much longer for each photon to be emitted. Therefore, the answer is **A.**

39.C This question can be done without calculations. We know that 4s is half of the half-life and so the activity must be more than 5000Bq. We know that the rate of decay is very fast at first and begins to slow down over time so there must be more activity lost in the first few seconds than the next few seconds so the answer must be 7100Bq and not 7500Bq, so the answer is **C**.

40.C By using Heisenberg uncertainty principle

$$\Delta x \Delta p \geq \frac{h}{4\pi}$$

$$\Delta p \geq \frac{h}{4\pi \Delta x}$$

$$\Delta p \geq \frac{6.63 \times 10^{-34}}{4\pi(10^{-15})}$$

This is approximately 5×10^{20} and so the answer is **C**.

1.A We know that

$$A\ (Area) = \pi r^2$$

Remember

$$If\ y = c^x, then\ \frac{\Delta y}{y} = x\frac{\Delta c}{c}$$

Applying the above formula to the first equation gives

$$\frac{\Delta A}{A}\ (fractional\ uncertainty\ in\ the\ area) = 2 \times \frac{\Delta r}{r}$$

Therefore, the answer is **A.**

2.C We know that

$$\Delta x \Delta p \geq \frac{h}{4\pi} \rightarrow \Delta p \geq \frac{h}{4\pi \Delta x}$$

Dividing both sides of the equation by p

$$\frac{\Delta p}{p} \geq \frac{h}{4p\pi\Delta x} = \frac{6.63 \times 10^{-34}}{4\pi \times 10^{-10} \times 10^{-20}} = 5.3 \times 10^{-5} \sim 5 \times 10^{-5}$$

Therefore, the answer is **C.**

3.B We know that

$$s = ut + \frac{1}{2}gt^2$$

$$80 = 0 + \frac{1}{2} \times 10t^2 \rightarrow t = 4.04\ s$$

During projectile motion, horizontal speed is constant, thus we can use the formula $Distance = speed \times time$ to find the distance from the bottom of the cliff to the point where the ball lands in the sea

$Distance = 15 \times 4.04 = 60.6\ m \sim 60\ m$

Therefore, the answer is **B.**

4.C Newton's third law states that every action has an equal and opposite reaction.
Golden Rule: In Newton's third law, if object A exerts a force on object B, then object B also exerts an equal and opposite force on object A (the action-reaction force has to be occurring between the same two objects)
The only choice that corresponds with this rule is option C. Therefore, the answer is **C.**

5.B We know that

$$(E_p) = mgh = 6.10 \times 10^2 \times 8.0 \sim 4880J = 4.88\ kJ$$

(since mg = weight, mg = $6.10 \times 10^2\ N$)
Golden Rule (for multiplication and division): The least number of significant figures in any number of the multiplication/division determines the number of significant figures in the answer. In this question 8.0 has the least number of significant figures (2) and thus, the final answer must have 2 significant figures (4.9 kJ)
Therefore, the answer is **B.**

6.A **[Remember]** Force is the rate of change of momentum. In other words,

$$F = \frac{\Delta P}{\Delta t}$$

Thus, the force can be found by finding the gradient of the graph at that time interval

$$Force\ for\ the\ first\ 2\ seconds = \frac{20-0}{2-0} = 10N$$

$$Force\ for\ the\ second\ 2\ seconds = \frac{20-20}{4-2} = 0N$$

Therefore, the answer is **A.**

7.A This questions tests your knowledge of the law of conservation of momentum. Since the initial momentum of the ball is 0, the final momentum of the ball is 0 as well. We know the formula $p = mv$ and so the momentum of the tennis ball is $3 \times 10^{-3} \times 10 = 3 \times 10^{-2}$. And so, the momentum of the gun should be the same in the opposite direction and so with that logic, we can find the velocity using the formula:

$$v = \frac{p}{m}$$

and so we have:

$$v = \frac{3 \times 10^{-2}}{0.6} = 0.05m/s$$

and so, the correct answer is option **A.**

8.D The way to do this question is by extending the lines in each of the options and seeing which one of them balance out all the forces (because this object is moving at constant velocity). Only in options C and D are the frictional force and normal force roughly equal and so we need to analyze further to see which one of those is the correct answer.

If you extend the normal reaction line (by the same distance as the original) and draw the equivalent of the frictional force line from the bottom of the weight line and see if they connect. This only works for the way lines are arranged in option **D**, and so it is the correct answer. See the image below for an illustration of the explanation above.

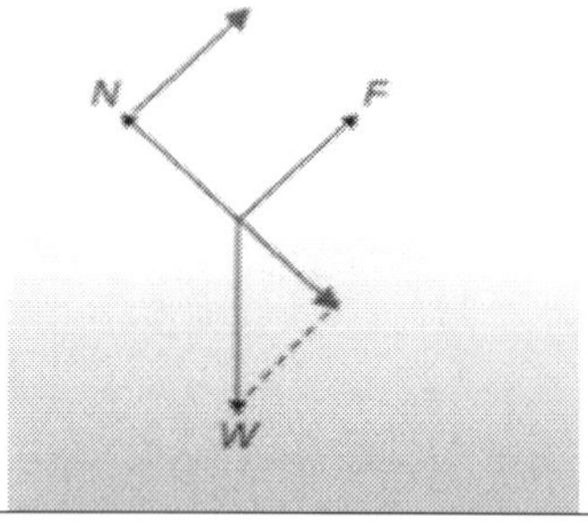

9.C **[Remember]** Total intermolecular potential energy of a substance increases when the molecules are farther apart. Phase change from solid to gas involves molecules moving farther apart, so there is an increase in the total intermolecular potential energy of the substance. Internal energy is defined as the total energy of a system (sum of random kinetic energy and inter-particle potential energy).

Since the question explicitly states that there is no change in temperature, there is no change in kinetic energy (remember that average kinetic energy is directly proportional to the temperature). However, there is an increase in the intermolecular potential energy (as molecules are farther apart in the gaseous state). This increase in potential energy leads to increase in the internal energy. Therefore, the answer is **C**.

10.C We know that

$$E_k = \frac{GMm}{2r}$$

We also know that

$$E_t = -\frac{GMm}{2r}$$

As satellite Y is at a higher orbit, r (distance between satellite and center of the Earth) is higher. Higher the value of r, smaller the kinetic energy (it becomes smaller according to the first equation) and higher the total energy (it becomes less negative according to the second equation). Therefore, the answer is **C**.

11.A We know that the formula for escape speed of a planet with radius R is

$$V_{esc} = \sqrt{\frac{2GM}{R}}$$

And the formula for orbital speed of a planet with radius R is

$$V_{orbit} = \sqrt{\frac{GM}{2R}}$$

where 2R is the radius of the orbit.

The ratio

$$\frac{V_{orbit}}{V_{esc}} = \frac{1}{2}$$

Therefore, $V_{orbit} = \frac{1}{2}V_{esc}$ and so the correct answer is option **A.**

12.D We know that

$$q = mc\Delta T$$

Since the question asks for rate at which thermal energy is transferred, let's divide both sides of the first equation by Δt (time taken for energy transfer)

$$\frac{q}{\Delta t} = \frac{mc\Delta T}{\Delta t}$$

The question tells us that the rate of change of the temperature of the liquid is k, thus, let's replace $\frac{\Delta T}{\Delta t}$ with k

$$\frac{q}{\Delta t} = kmc$$

Therefore, the answer is **D.**

13.A Note: These kinds of absurd questions will pop up in every paper 1, so do read the Nature of Science section of every chapter in your physics textbook.

Empirical evidence is data acquired by observation/means of senses. All the three gas laws are empirical since they are capable of being verified by observation and thus, $\frac{pV}{T} = constant$ is also verified by observation (i.e., empirical). This is why sometimes the gas laws are referred to as empirical gas laws. Significant relationships between the nature of gas samples have been derived empirically (through observation rather than an attempt to explicate a theory). Therefore, the correct answer is option **A.**

Golden Rule: The only way to answer these questions is to read the Nature of Science section of every chapter in your physics textbook, so don't ignore them!

14.A We know the formula

$$pV = nRT$$

When the valve is closed, the equation for cylinder X is

$$p_x V = nRT = 3RT$$

And so, the pressure is

$$p_x = \frac{3RT}{V}$$

For cylinder Y,

$$p_y \frac{V}{2} = nRT = 2RT$$

After the valve is opened, the equation will be

$$p\left(V + \frac{V}{2}\right) = nRT = (3 + 2)RT = 5RT$$

$$p\left(\frac{3V}{2}\right) = 5RT$$

$$p = \frac{10}{3}RT$$

Change of pressure in X is

$$p - p_x = \frac{10}{3}RT - \frac{3RT}{V} = \frac{RT}{3V} = +\frac{1}{3}\left(\frac{RT}{V}\right)$$

Therefore, the correct answer is option **A.**

15.C The formula for time period is

$$T = \frac{1}{f}$$

and we can calculate the frequency using

$$c = f\lambda \text{ and so } f = \frac{c}{\lambda}$$

The wavelength of the wave is 1.5m as can be obtained from the graph and the speed has been given as 0.5m/s and so the frequency is

$$f = \frac{0.5}{1.5} = \frac{1}{3}$$

and so the time period is

$$T = \frac{1}{\frac{1}{3}} = 3$$

Therefore, the time period is 3s and so the answer is option **C.**

16.A We can see that the graph is a negative cosine curve, and we know the formula

$$x = x_0 sin(\omega t)$$

In trigonometry we know that $sin(90 - \theta) = cos(\theta)$ and thus,

$$-cos\theta = sin(\theta - 90)$$

Therefore, there is an initial phase change of $\frac{\pi}{2}$ that we need to account for in the first equation. The first equation becomes

$$x = x_o \sin\left(\omega t - \frac{\pi}{2}\right)$$

We know that

$$\omega = \frac{2\pi}{time\ period} = \frac{2\pi}{2T} = \frac{\pi}{T}$$

We know that maximum displacement, x_0, is 2A from the graph.

Substituting the value ω back in the first equation gives us

$$x = 2Asin\left(\frac{\pi}{T}t - \frac{\pi}{2}\right)$$

Now let us find the derivative of displacement to find the velocity

$$v = \frac{dx}{dt} = 2Acos\left(\frac{\pi}{T}t - \frac{\pi}{2}\right) \times \frac{\pi}{T} = \frac{2\pi A}{T}\cos\left(\frac{\pi}{T}t - \frac{\pi}{2}\right)$$

We know that $\cos(\theta - 90) = -sin\theta$ and therefore,

$$v = -\frac{2\pi A}{T}\sin\left(\frac{\pi}{T}t\right)$$

Therefore, the correct answer is option **A.**

Golden tip: Do remember your math concepts (especially trigonometric identities) for your physics exams as there are many questions that can be done using the concept.

17.D We know that

$$a = -\omega^2 x$$

Looking at the above equation we can make 3 deductions:

- The graph has to be a straight line since the equation has the form y = mx + x, where m = $-\omega^2$ and c = 0
- $-\omega^2$ (the gradient of the graph) signifies that the line slopes downwards (the gradient is negative)
- Since the equation has y-intercept (c) = 0, it can be deduced that the line passes through the origin

The only graph that corresponds with these 3 fairly obvious deductions is option **D.**

Therefore, the answer is **D.**

18.B The formula for intensity is $I = I_0\cos^2\theta$. Therefore, we can substitute values of θ to find the value of I and we get:

$$\theta = 0 \rightarrow I = 1$$

$$\theta = 90 \rightarrow I = 0$$

$$\theta = 180 \rightarrow I = 1$$

$$\theta = 270 \rightarrow I = 0$$

$$\theta = 360 \rightarrow I = 1$$

From these values, we can clearly see that the answer is the graph shown in option **B.**

19.D We know that the node happens at the closed end of the pipe and so the node lies in the surface of the water (realize that this is just a pipe closed at one end and open at the other). As more water is added, the length of the pipe decreases and so the wavelength of the harmonic motion also decreases. Since we know that $f = \frac{c}{\lambda}$ as λ decreases the f increases and so the answer is option **D**.

20.C A third-harmonic wave in a string closed at both ends is one that has 4 nodes and there are 1.5 oscillations of the wave. So, if we imagine the diagram, we can see that distance between two consecutive nodes will be half of the wavelength which is 0.4m. Since the two points in the question are distanced by 0.6m which is more than 0.4m the two points are in antiphase which means that they have a phase difference of π thus leading to option **C** being the correct answer.

21.A Since the train is approaching the observer, the formula for f' is

$$f' = f\left(\frac{v}{v - u_s}\right)$$

and so, as the u_s decreases, the frequency also decreases. Moreover, the intensity does not depend on the frequency and so the intensity does not change. Therefore, the answer is option **D**.

22.A The filter only changes the intensity and so there is no change to the angular separation or the resolution of the images. Therefore, the answer is option **A**.

23.B The first equation

$$V = \frac{W}{q} \rightarrow W = Vq$$

According to the question, charge $(q) = ne$

Replacing q with ne in the first equation:

$$W = neV$$

Therefore, the answer is **B.**

24.C The first equation (d is the diameter of the wire)

$$\rho = \frac{RA}{L}$$

$$\rightarrow R = \frac{L \times \rho}{A}$$

$$\rightarrow R = \frac{L \times \rho}{\pi \times \left(\frac{d}{2}\right)^2}$$

$$\rightarrow R = \frac{4L\rho}{\pi \times (d)^2}$$

$$\rightarrow \frac{1}{R} = \frac{\pi \times (d)^2}{4L\rho}$$

In order to obtain a straight line, we need our equation of the graph to be in the form $y = mx + c$. In the equation

$\frac{1}{R} = \frac{\pi \times (d)^2}{4L\rho}$

- $y = \frac{1}{R}$
- $m = \frac{\pi}{4L\rho}$ *(constant)*
- $x = d^2$

Thus, $diameter^2$ should be plotted on the x-axis and $\frac{1}{Resistance}$ should be plotted on the y axis. Therefore, the answer is **C.**

25.D Resistance of parallel circuit:

$$\frac{1}{R} = \frac{1}{6} + \frac{1}{6} = \frac{1}{3} \rightarrow R = 3\Omega$$

$\textit{The total resistance of the circuit } (R_t) = 3 + 1 = 4\Omega$

$$\textit{Current passing through the circuit} = \frac{V}{R_t} = \frac{12}{4} = 3A$$

However, we actually need to calculate the voltage across the two resistors connected in parallel and so we use the formula $V = IR$ to get

$$V = 3 \times 3 = 9V$$

Therefore, the correct answer is option **D.**

Note: this question plays a trick in the mind of the candidates and makes them think that the voltage is being measured across the 1Ω resistor, or even the whole circuit for that matter. But if you look closely, since current flows from the positive terminal to the negative terminal, the current has not actually flown to the 1Ω resistor at the time the voltage is being measured. Therefore, the voltage measured is the voltage across the 2 resistors in parallel.

26.A In the diagram shown in the question, the diodes allow current to pass through them in two directions. Therefore, this reflects a full-wave rectification.

[Memorize] In full-wave rectification, the output is positive during negative half-cycles of the input wave. On the contrary, in half-wave rectification, the output is 0 during negative half-cycles of the input wave.

Since the diagram represents full-wave rectification we can eliminate option C and D. We know that the time period is 20ms which is the time taken for one complete wave (which is also the same time taken for the completion of two half-cycles). This is only reflected in option A where one half-cycle occurs in 10ms. Thus, option **A** is the correct answer,

27.B For capacitors connected in series arrangement:

$$\frac{1}{C_{series}} = \frac{1}{C_1} + \frac{1}{C_2} + \ldots$$

$$\frac{1}{\left(\frac{1}{9}\right)} = \frac{1}{C} + \frac{1}{C} + \frac{1}{C}$$

$$9 = \frac{3}{C}$$

$$C = \frac{3}{9} = \frac{1}{3} mF$$

For capacitors connected in parallel arrangement:

$C_{parallel} = C_1 + C_2 + C_3$

$C_{parallel} = \frac{1}{3} + \frac{1}{3} + \frac{1}{3} = 1mF$

Therefore, the answer is **B.**

28.D We know the very useful formula:

$$\frac{\varepsilon_p}{\varepsilon_s} = \frac{N_p}{N_s} = \frac{I_s}{I_p}$$

And so, we can substitute the values we know to find to find the number of turns in the secondary coil:

$$\frac{600}{N_s} = \frac{240}{12} \rightarrow N_s = 30$$

Now, we can find the power output $I_{rms} \times V_{rms} = 0.6 \times 240 = 144W$ and we know that the power input is 120W. The efficiency is calculated by dividing the total output power and then total input power: $\frac{120}{144} = 0.83$ and so the efficiency is 83%. Thus, the correct answer is option **D.**

29.C Lenz's law states that the induced current is such that it opposes the change that causes it. The coil on the left side moves such that there is a higher area of the magnetic field that it covers and so the magnetic flux increases. This means that the induced current should be into the paper and so the field is clockwise by using the right-hand rule. The opposite effect happens for the coil on the right side as the current is out of the paper and the field is anti-clockwise. Therefore, the correct answer is option **C.**

30.D A and C are equipotential points and so the electron has the same amount of potential energy at those points. Recognize that the positive side is on the right of the page (since electric field is from positive to negative) and so when the point is at D and moves to B, a part of its potential energy is converted to kinetic energy which means that the object has higher potential energy when it is at point **D.**

31.D The formula for force acting on the particle because of the electric field is $F = qE$. The formula for force acting on the particle because of the magnetic field is

$$F = qvBsin(90) = qvB$$

Since there is no deflection of the proton, let us equate the two equations and we get

$$qE = qvB$$

And so,

$$E = vB$$

This tells us that the charge gets cancelled out and so both the electron and the alpha particle are not deflected. Therefore, the correct answer is option **D.**

32.D We know that (Remember that ω is angular velocity)

$$F = \frac{mv^2}{r} = m\omega^2 r = 0.02\ \times\ 3\pi\ \times \frac{1}{2} = 0.09\pi^2\ N$$

Centripetal force always acts towards the center of the circle, so the direction of force is towards center of circle. Therefore, the answer is **D.**

33.A In a β^+ decay, a proton is transformed into a neutron inside the nucleus of an atom. Therefore, the atomic number (Z) decreases by 1 (becomes Z – 1).
[Memorize] Instead of emitting an electron, a β^+ decay emits a positron (a β^- decay emits an electron). A β^- decay emits an anti-neutrino particle while β^+ decay emits a neutrino particle.
Therefore, the answer is **A.**

Note: Paper 1 Questions in atomic, nuclear and quantum physics involve a lot of memorization and focuses on minor details, so please learn every intricate detail in your physics book and make notes. I would highly recommend the Tsokos physics HL textbook for atomic, nuclear and quantum physics as it covers all essential information in great depth

34.C In the data booklet, we can see that π^+ consists of u and $\bar{d}$ and has a charge $+1\left(\frac{2}{3}+\frac{1}{3}\right)$. The question asks for the quark structure of π^-, which has a charge -1.

Option A: $ud\left(\frac{2}{3}-\frac{1}{3}= +\frac{1}{3}\right)$

Option B: $u\bar{d}\left(\frac{2}{3}+\frac{1}{3}= +1\right)$

Option C: $\bar{u}d\left(-\frac{2}{3}-\frac{1}{3}= -1\right)$

Option D: $\bar{u}\bar{d}\left(-\frac{2}{3}+\frac{1}{3}= -\frac{1}{3}\right)$

Only option C ($\bar{u}d$) has a charge -1. Therefore, the answer is **C**

35.C So, let us check individually for the conservation of each. The charge on the left side is 0 and the charge on the right side is also 0 (because there is one positive and one negative) and so charge is conserved. The baryon number on the left side is one while the baryon number for the right side is 0 and so the baryon number is not conserved. Lastly, there are 0 leptons on the left side of the equation while there is one lepton in the right side of the equation and so lepton number is not conserved either. Therefore, the correct answer is option **C.**

36.B The main role of a moderator in a nuclear fission reactor is to slow down neutrons, hence there is a decrease in kinetic energy of the neutron. Slowing down the neutrons makes them more effective in the fission chain reaction. The fission chain reaction will continue at a constant rate. A slow neutron can be easily captured by the uranium-235 nucleus while a fast neutron will not be captured easily. Hence, there is an increase in the probability that this neutron can cause nuclear fission. Therefore, the answer is **B.**

37.D The value of the solar constant is $1.36 \times 10^3 Wm^{-2}$. The intensity is inversely proportional to the square of the radius (which we know using $I \propto x^{-2}$ [Topic 4.3] from the data booklet) and so if we apply the ratios here:

$$I_{venus}:I_{earth} = R^2_{earth}:R^2_{venus}$$

$$I_{venus} = I_{earth} \times (1.5)^2 = 1.36 \times 10^3 \times (1.5)^2 = 3060Wm^{-2} = 3kWm^{-2}$$

Therefore, the answer is **D.**

38.B Recall that:

$$E = hf$$

As the frequency is increased, energy of emitted electrons increases (h is plank's constant).

Moreover, intensity is dependent on the number of photons per second as well as the energy of each photon. Since the energy of photons increase, but the intensity remains constant, we need the number of photons per second to decrease for that to happen. If a smaller number of photons reach the metal per second, then less electrons are emitted per second. This makes option **B** the correct answer.

39.D **[Memorise]**

Bohr model for hydrogen:

- Bohr's model suggests that electron in the hydrogen atom has discrete or quantized energy (this is proven through the equation $E = -\frac{13.6}{n^2}eV$)
- In the process of calculation, Bohr assumed that the angular momentum is quantized
- The assumption of quantization of angular momentum allowed Bohr to prove that the radii of electron's orbits (orbital radius) are also quantized (this is proven through the equation $r = \frac{h^2}{4\pi^2 ke^2 m} \times n^2$)

Therefore, the answer is **D.**

Golden Rule: Paper 1 questions in quantum physics may seem very absurd and usually involve a lot of memorization and limited logic when compared to questions from other chapters. The only way to crack such types of MCQs is to read the quantum physics chapter in your physics textbook very closely and make note of every intricate detail. I would highly recommend the Tsokos Physics HL textbook for quantum physics as it covers all essential information in great depth.

40.B **[Remember]** The nucleus exists in discrete energy levels. The evidence for this existence stems from the notion that the energies the gamma ray photons emitted by nuclei in gamma decay are discrete. In addition, note that in beta decays, electron has a continuous range of energies (not discrete) and in alpha decays, energies of alpha particles emitted by the nuclei are discrete. Therefore, the answer is **B.**

1.D If we write down the formula for each of the quantities and calculate their units, for pressure we get:

$$Pressure = \frac{Force}{Area} = \frac{ma}{area} = \frac{kgms^{-2}}{m^2} = kgm^{-1}s^{-2}$$

And therefore, the answer is option **D.**

2.C So as the velocity increases, the varying force towards the left side increases until it matches the constant force acting towards the right side. When they become equal, then the acceleration becomes 0 and so the velocity becomes constant (which again means that the varying force will not change) and so the velocity increases from 0 to a maximum and stays there. Therefore, the answer is option **C.**

3.B Using the formula

$$s = ut + \frac{1}{2}at^2$$

we can substitute the values of time to find the displacement and so we get:

After 1 second: $s = \frac{1}{2} * 10 * 1^2 = 5$

After 2 seconds: $s = \frac{1}{2} * 10 * 2^2 = 20$

After 3 seconds: $s = \frac{1}{2} * 10 * 3^2 = 45$

After 4 seconds: $s = \frac{1}{2} * 10 * 4^2 = 80$

Therefore, in the first second the object travels 5m, and then in the next second it travels 15m (20 – 5) and then in the next second travels 25m (45 – 20) and then 35m (80 – 45) in the last second. Therefore, the correct answer is option **B.**

4.D The horizontal component is constant and essentially we need to know the time of flight to find the displacement. To find the time we need the vertical component which needs to be found out from the angle of throwing and the height of the cliff. Therefore, we need all the three pieces of information and so the answer is option **D.**

5.C We know that the change in velocity can be found out by calculating the area under an acceleration-time graph. The graph can be split into one rectangle and one trapezium (or two rectangles and a triangle) and the total area adds up to 10m/s which makes **C** the correct answer.

6.A First let us convert $10^8 ev$ to Joules:

$$10^8 \times 1.6 \times 10^{-19} = 1.6 \times 10^{-11}\ \mathrm{J}$$

So, for the particle to have that much energy we need $\frac{1}{2}mv^2 = 1.6 \times 10^{-11}$ and so:

$$v^2 = \frac{2 \times 1.6 \times 10^{-11}}{32 \times 10^{-3}} = 10^{-9}$$

which means that $v = 10^{-3}$ and so the correct answer is option **A.**

7.D The force when the extension is x is kx and while the extension is $\frac{x}{4}$ the force is $\frac{kx}{4}$. The work done is calculated by the difference in the area in both cases and so the area under the graph in the first case is $\frac{1}{2}kx \times x = \frac{1}{2}kx^2 = E$ and for the second case it is

$$\frac{1}{2} \cdot \frac{kx}{4} \cdot \frac{x}{4} = \frac{1}{2}\frac{kx^2}{16} = \frac{E}{16}$$

Therefore, if we calculate the difference we will get $E - \frac{E}{16}$ and so the answer is $\frac{15E}{16}$ which is option **D.**

8.A The water is initially at 290K and at the end it becomes 273K (which is 0 degrees Celsius). Using the conservation of energy (i.e., the heat lost by water is equal to the heat gained by the ice) and so we have: $mc(290 - 273) = ML$ where **M** is the mass of the ice. We can rearrange to get: $M = \frac{mc(17)}{L}$ and so the answer is option **A.**

9.D **[Memorize]** The conditions for being an ideal gas are low pressure and low density and so the correct answer is option **D.**

10.C To find the ratio of mass, we need to find the ratio of the number of moles which can be found out using the formula: $pV = nRT$ and so we can rearrange it to get $nR = \frac{pV}{T}$ and so since R is the same for both P and Q, we need to find the ratio:

$$\frac{\frac{pV_P}{T_P}}{\frac{pV_Q}{T_Q}} = \frac{\frac{p(2V)}{200}}{\frac{p(V)}{400}} = \frac{2V}{200} \cdot \frac{400}{V} = 4$$

And so, the correct answer is option **C.**

11.C Since the frequency is 25Hz and the velocity is 100m/s, we know that the wavelength is 4m. The horizontal distance between X and Z is essentially $\frac{3}{4}\lambda$ and so the distance is 3m between the two points. In conclusion, this means that the answer is option **C.**

12.C From the graph, the maximum displacement can be seen to be 2 micrometers and the time period of 1 oscillation is 20×10^{-6} and so the frequency is $\frac{1}{T} = \frac{1}{20 \times 10^{-6}} = 50kHz$ and so the answer is option **C.**

13.C We know that the intensity is dependent on the value of $\cos^2 \theta$ and so the values of θ where $cos\theta$ is maximum are 0, 180, 360, 540, 720 and so options C and D both have these values but since the question asks for the first three **consecutive** values, the correct answer will be option **C.**

14.B We know that for the first harmonic in a pipe open on one side the length of the pipe is equal to a quarter of the wavelength: $L = \frac{\lambda}{4}$ and for the second harmonic it is $L = \frac{3\lambda}{4}$. Now, if we substitute the values we have to find the wavelength we have 2.4m for the first harmonic and 0.8m for the second harmonic. Now, we can find $f = \frac{v}{\lambda}$ and so we have:

$\frac{300}{2.4} = 125Hz$ for the first harmonic and $\frac{300}{0.8} = 375Hz$ for the second harmonic and so the correct answer is option **B.**

15.A Since the weight of the object does not change, we need the electric force (qE) to decrease (as the charge needs to move downwards and we know that mg is pulling it down and the qE is pulling it upwards) and so we know that $E = \frac{V}{d}$ where d is the distance between the plates. For E to decrease, we want the distance between the plates to increase (which isn't any of the options). The other way to reduce qE is by reducing the charge and this is indeed option **A** which is the correct answer.

16.B If we want current to be 0, we need the potential difference across the 3Ω resistor should be equal to the emf across P and so this question is testing you on potential divider. Since we know $V = IR$, we have:

$$24 \cdot \frac{3}{3+9} = \frac{24}{4} = 6V$$

and so the correct answer is option **B.**

17.D If we apply Fleming's left hand rule where the thumb is F, the index finger is B and the middle finger is I, we can see that if we have a plane where one side is the index finger and the other side is the middle finger, the thumb is pointing upwards while the plane is lying flat. Therefore, in other words, the force is perpendicular to the plane containing B and I and so the answer is option **D.**

18.A The object is undergoing horizontal circular motion. Let us divide the tension into its individual perpendicular components. The vertical component is $Tcos\theta$ while the horizontal component is $Tsin\theta$. We know that the $Tcos\theta$ is balanced by mg and that $Tsin\theta$ is $m\omega^2 r$ as this is centripetal force. Now if we find the ratio of $Tcos\theta$ to $Tsin\theta$ we have:

$$\frac{Tsin\theta}{Tcos\theta} = \frac{m\omega^2 r}{mg} = \frac{\omega^2 r}{g}$$

Therefore, the correct answer is option **A.**

19.B We know that in a beta-minus decay, a neutron is converted into a proton and an electron and the electron leaves the nucleus. This means that the mass number remains the same and the atomic number increases by 1. Therefore, since X undergoes beta decay to form R, we know that X and R have the same mass number and so the correct answer is option **B.**

20.A The charge of proton is +1e, the charge of electron is -1e, and the charge of an alpha particle is +2e. The mass of a proton is 1 amu, the mass of an electron is 1/1836 amu while the mass of an alpha particle is 4 amu. From this we can clearly see that the largest charge to mass ratio is that of an electron because its mass is very low. For the mass to charge ratio, we can see that the ratio is 1 for a proton while it is 0.5 for an alpha particle and so alpha particle has the lowest ratio. Therefore, the correct answer is option **A.**

21.B Note that Gamma radiation doesn't have charge and consequently, they are not affected by electric or magnetic fields. However they affect a photographic plate, and their effect is greater than that of beta rays. They cause fluorescence when they strike a fluorescent material. Moreover gamma rays are created by nuclear decay inside a nucleus (hence, option C is wrong). Therefore the answer is **B.**

22.D Equations of motion for objects in uniform acceleration are scientific equations that were modelled through the study of real-life motion and are only applicable when the acceleration when if the acceleration is constant. Moreover keep in mind that Newton's laws of motion is are used to relate forces to other quantities in mechanics and NOT equations of motion. Therefore, the answer is **D.**

Note: These types of questions are based on the Nature of Science portion of your Tsokos textbook, so please read them beforehand. Also note that you can find the equations of motion for uniform acceleration in the IB Physics data booklet.

23.B Specific energy is the energy per unit mass ($J\ kg^{-1}$)
Energy density is the energy stored per unit volume ($J\ m^{-3}$)
Therefore, the answer is **B.**

24.A During nuclear fission, neutrons are released with high kinetic energy at a great speed. The role of moderators is to slow down the neutrons when they collide with the moderator nuclei so that the neutrons can be captured by the Uranium-235 to sustain the chain reaction. Slowing down the neutrons directly corresponds to a decrease in kinetic energy; hence the function of a moderator is to decrease the kinetic energy of the neutrons emitted. Therefore, the answer is **A.**

25.C Let's look at the formula for albedo,

$$Albedo = \frac{total\ scattered\ radiation}{total\ incident\ radiation}$$

We know from the question that the value of albedo is 0.1 $\left(\frac{10}{100}\right)$

This means that of all the incident radiation, about 10% is reflected by the moon's surface. Therefore, the answer is **C.**

26.A This question is a trick question. A lot of tricky questions give you additional unnecessary information to confuse you. You must learn to disregard such information and only consider relevant data, which is an essential skill. In this question, we know from our knowledge of Simple Harmonic Motion, that velocity is 0 at the amplitude (maximum displacement). Therefore, the answer is **A.**

27.A We know that the formula for angle between first diffraction minimum and central maximum,

$$\theta = \frac{\lambda}{b} = \frac{v}{fb}$$

where λ is wavelength, f is frequency, v is the velocity of light and b is slit width

Note that the velocity of light and size of the slit are constant (obviously!)

This means that the angle between first diffraction minimum and central maximum is <u>inversely proportional</u> to the frequency.

Now based on the above finding, we can devise a new formula,

$$\frac{\theta_1}{\theta_2} = \frac{f_1}{f_2} = \frac{500}{750} = \frac{2}{3}$$

$$\theta_2 = \frac{2}{3} \times 2.4 \times 10^{-3} = 1.6 \times 10^{-3}\, rad$$

Therefore, the answer is **A.**

28.C For a diffraction grating of spacing d, the angle between the central maxima and the nth order maxima is given by

$$dsin(\theta) = n\lambda$$

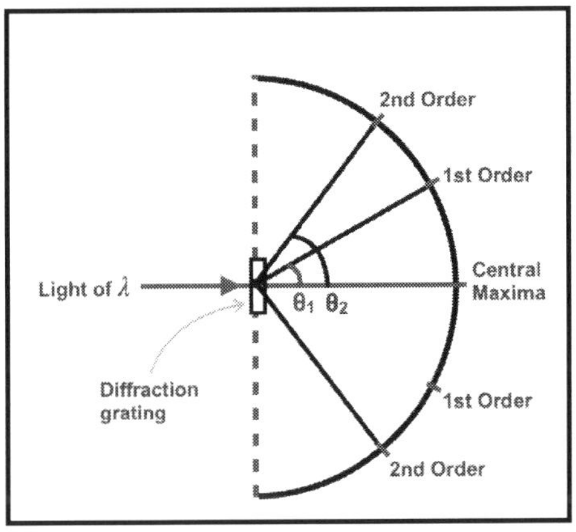

We can substitute values into the above equation to get

$$3\lambda sin\theta = 2\lambda$$

And so,

$$sin\theta = \frac{2}{3}$$

Which means that

$$\theta = \sin^{-1}\frac{2}{3}$$

But since this value is the angle from the central to the maxima on top (refer to diagram above) and we are required to find the angle between the two second order maximum points which requires us to multiply our value by 2. Therefore, the correct answer is option **C**.

29.B The sea waves can be treated as coming from a fixed source and surfer as a moving observer. Since the surfboard crosses the wave fronts with a frequency of 0.4 Hz, which is higher than the frequency of sea waves as they arrive at the beach, we can conclude that the observer is moving towards the waves. Since she is moving towards the waves, she is essentially moving away from the beach. By applying doppler effect formula

$$f' = \frac{f(v + u_0)}{v}$$

Where $f' = 0.4$ and $f = 0.1$ and $v = 2.0$. We can find u_0 by

$$\frac{0.4}{0.1} = \frac{2 + u_0}{2}$$

And this means that

$$u_0 = 8 - 2 = 6$$

Therefore, the speed of the surfboard relative to the beach is $6.0m/s$ and thus, the correct answer is option **B**.

30.D Gravitational potential at a point on the surface is given by

$$Potential = \frac{-GM}{R}$$

where **R** is the distance from the centre of the planet, **G** is the gravitational constant and **M** is the mass. We know that,

$$V = \frac{-GM}{2R}$$

where **R** is the radius of the planet.

In the above equation, the denominator is nothing but the sum of the radius of the planet and the distance above the surface of the planet (which is also equal to the radius of the planet).

Gravitational potential a distance $2R$ above the surface of the planet,

$$V_2 = \frac{-GM}{3R}$$

From the above equations, it is fairly straightforward to deduce that,

$$V_2 = \frac{2V}{3}$$

Therefore, the answer is **D**.

31.C Electrostatic force between 2-point charges,

$$F = \frac{kq_1q_2}{x^2}$$

where q_1 and q_2 are the two charges, x is the distance between the charges and k is the coulomb constant. Once the distance between the charges is increased to 3x, the new force,

$$F_2 = \frac{kq_1q_2}{(3x)^2} = \frac{kq_1q_2}{9x^2} = \frac{F}{9}$$

Therefore, the answer is **C**.

32.B The electron will experience a force in the vertical direction and continues to move with velocity v in the horizontal direction. This force is going to make the electron move in a parabolic path. Therefore, the answer is **B**.

33.C First let us understand the question. Coil Y has a direct current and coil X is moved towards Y. The question asks us the direction of current induced in X as it moves towards and away from Y. The current carrying coil Y has a magnetic field around it and when seen from the direction of X, the current is in clockwise direction. Using the right-hand grip rule, the north pole is pointing in the direction away from X and towards Y (essentially towards the right side of the page). If X is moved towards Y, the change in flux will cause a current to be induced in coil X and by applying Lenz's law, we notice that the south pole of coil X will be next to the south pole of coil Y. Using right-hand grip rule we can see that the direction of current will be in the opposite direction to that of coil Y.

When the coil X moves away from coil Y, the exact opposite phenomenon happens and so, the direction of induced current is in the same direction as the current in coil Y. Therefore, the correct answer is option **C**.

34.B Faraday's law states that magnitude of induced emf is directly proportional to the rate of change of magnetic flux,

$$\varepsilon = -\frac{d\Phi}{dt}$$

where Φ is flux and t is time. We also know that,

$$\Phi = \Phi \sin(\omega t)$$

Now let us find an expression for the emf using the formula above,

$$\varepsilon = -\frac{d\Phi}{dt} = -\Phi \cos(\omega t)$$

From the two expressions above, it is clear that the induced emf lags the magnetic flux by a phase of $\frac{\pi}{2}$

Therefore, the answer is **B**.

Note: You can also deduce the answer by looking at the shape of the graph and using some Math knowledge. We know that sine graph starts at the origin and negative cosine graph starts below the x-axis, making B the answer.

35.C From the data booklet, we know that,

$$V = \frac{Q}{C}$$

where V is voltage, Q is charge and C is capacitance

Let us calculate the voltage,

$$V = \frac{15 \times 10^{-6}}{1.0 \times 10^{-6}} = 15\,V$$

When the capacitor is connected across the resistor, it is going to discharge, and maximum current occurs when it first starts to discharge

We can calculate that current using,

$$I = \frac{V}{R} = \frac{15}{25} = 0.6A$$

Therefore, the answer is **C**.

36.A Diodes Q and S conduct when current flows from **M** to N. Diodes P and R conduct when current flows in the opposite direction. The direction of conventional current through resistor is from right to left in both situations. Therefore, the answer is **A**.

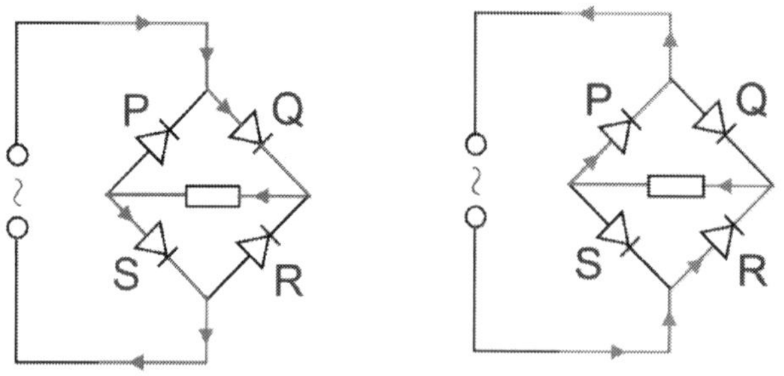

37.A **[Memorize]** Quantum tunnelling is the quantum mechanical phenomenon where a wavefunction can propagate through a potential barrier. A particle with lower energy can pass through a potential barrier with a higher energy level. Therefore, the answer is **A**.

Tip: Please learn all definitions in the Tsokos textbook thoroughly.

38.B We know the de Broglie equation,

$$\lambda = \frac{h}{\rho}$$

where λ is wavelength, ρ is the momentum of photon and h is plank's constant Doubling the intensity doubles the number of photons in the beam of radiation. Since the frequency remains the same, the energy and wavelength of the photon is unchanged. Hence, based on the equation above, the momentum of the photon remains as ρ. Therefore, the answer is **B.**

39.B Particle behaviour of electron is evidenced by the electron being emitted from a metal surface due to photoelectric effect and the electron oscillating to-and-fro in a conductor due to time-varying electric currents (which causes electrons to accelerate and emit radio waves). However, the electron diffraction that occurs when the electron interacts with an atom is an evidence for the wave nature of an electron, NOT the particle nature. Therefore, the answer is **B.**

40.A The decay rate of a radioactive material, which is also referred to as activity, is the number of nuclides that decay per unit time. On the other hand, the law of radioactive decay suggests that the decay rate (activity) is directly proportional to the number of nuclides present ($A = \lambda N$). At time t, the number of undecayed nuclide is N (stated in the question). Hence, decay rate is proportional to N. Therefore, the answer is **A.**

Paper 1 Success Strategies

I would personally describe the IB Physics HL paper 1 examination as tricky rather than difficult. Here are 8 general tips that will help you attain success in this paper:

1. **Prioritize specific topics**. If you have done paper 1 past papers, you must have noticed that there are far more questions tested on Mechanics and Quantum Physics when compared to other chapters. You certainly don't want to be spending too much time on trivial topics (at least with regard to paper 1) such as Circular motion and Gravitation where barely 1 to 2 questions are tested. Therefore, spend time mastering Mechanics and Quantum Physics by thoroughly reading the Tsokos Physics textbook and attempting the problems given in the end of the corresponding chapters. Keep in mind that the questions asked from Quantum Physics mainly test your mastery of the content directly presented in the textbook (there are minimal application questions from this topic), so a close reading of the Quantum Physics chapter should help you score good marks in that section
2. **Attempt ALL the questions**. Note that there is no penalty for incorrect responses. Even if you don't know the correct response, you should be able to eliminate some of the obviously incorrect solutions (referred to as the 'distractors'), increasing the probability of selecting the correct response. Make sure you attempt every single question whatsoever. Every guess is worth it!
3. **Master all the equations.** After attempting countless IB Physics HL paper 1 questions, I have figured out a repetitive pattern that is common across all the papers. Usually, 50 to 60% of the paper tests your knowledge of identifying the right physics equation and using basic mathematics to compute some value. Most students struggle to complete the Paper 1 on time mainly because they don't know which equation to use after reading a question and consequently, end up spending a lot of precious time searching for the right equation in the data booklet. Yes, most of the questions will overwhelm you with values of different variables and will test your ability to form a connection between those variables and identify the right physics equation. Therefore, simply master all the physics equations in the textbook and try applying them to different questions. **Never rely on the data booklet**. Enter the exam hall with the assumption that a data booklet never exists. Moreover, enhance your basic arithmetic

skills as that will help you ease through basic math calculations, which can sometimes get really annoying. Arithmetically, you should be adept at dealing with powers of 10 quickly. You should also be able to work with ratios and combine 2 or more equations efficiently. **Stop relying on a calculator and sharpen your mental arithmetic!** I promise that if you spend time accentuating your arithmetic skills, you should find minimal difficulty finishing the paper

4. **The devil is in the detail!** Read every word of the question and don't ever ignore any detail. Noticing small details is the key to success in paper 1. Many questions in the paper will try to trick you by presenting unnecessary information and making the question appear so complicated and daunting. A small hidden detail is sometimes enough to deduce the answer. Read the question carefully and visualize the situation. Scouring the data booklet immediately after reading the question without spending enough time understanding the intricacies of the question can make students fall into traps. I would highly recommend you **highlight or underline key words and phrases in the question**. The wording of every question is highly significant
5. **Develop strategies for spotting the correct answer**. **Train your eyes!** Some of the general strategies for increasing your chances of getting the correct answer includes the following:
    - Eliminate the obviously incorrect solutions (sometimes they are so obviously wrong)
    - Pay close attention to units (this is very important as many questions test units and incorrect options trick you with wrong units)
    - Use units to attach meaning to the gradient of a graph and area under the graph. Make sure you look the axis of the graph and note the units
    - Master trigonometry! Many questions test sines, cosines, and tangents. Sometime Math HL knowledge can make your life much easier (especially in questions where you have to identify the correct trigonometric graph)
    - Don't jump to the data booklet. Understand the question and visualize the presented scenario
    - Finally, make an educated guess and attempt every single question

6. **Don't memorize. Understand and Apply!** As mentioned in the Physics guide, you should be aware that 50% of the questions require higher order thinking skills, so memorizing is not going to get you anywhere. How to enhance higher order thinking skills? By reading the textbook closely and applying key concepts in challenging questions. I highly recommend the Tsokos Cambridge Physics HL textbook as it explains concepts in great depth and detail
7. **Practice, Practice and Practice!** The internet is filled with resources. Firstly, practice all the past year exam questions as they will give you a good idea of what to expect in the examination. **Practice with timing**. One of the main challenges that students face during the paper 1 examination is timing and the only way to overcome that challenge is to practice as many papers as possible (with timing of course). Practice a huge variety of questions. If you are done with all IB past year questions, try A-Level paper 1 questions (which are extremely similar to IB questions and almost as difficult). Moreover, to gain conceptual understanding of topics, attempt questions in the Tsokos textbook that are found in the end of each chapter. Learn from your mistakes. Practice makes man perfect!
8. **Be confident.** Believe in yourself and remove the word 'stress' from your dictionary. Tension will only inhibit your ability to think. IB Physics paper 1 questions are tricky, and this is clearly reflected in the grade thresholds. Usually even a score of 28 out of 40 can earn you grade '7'. You can miss out 12 to 14 questions and still get a 7! Yes, you read that correctly, that is how tolerant the grade boundaries are. So, believe in yourself and be focused during the exam and you should be fine, trust me.

All the best!

Physics IA Success Strategies

The Physics IA can be a real struggle. You have to come up with a good topic to explore, design an experiment and then produce a detailed exploration around it. Phew! Chances are, if you are reading this, one or more of these stages are causing problems for you. Or maybe you haven't started on your IA yet, and the whole process looks daunting.

Don't worry. The Physics IA is not as hard as you think. This guide will enlighten you with success strategies that **we** used to earn a grade '7'. Follow this advice and trust me, you are going to do fine.

Shortlisting the right topic

Shortlisting the right IA topic is one of the most important aspects of your Physics IA journey. Most people struggle to come up with an appropriate topic (including myself a year ago). There are some students who don't have trust in themselves and think they are not well-equipped to carry out complex and intellectual investigations. Consequently, they end up choosing investigations that are far too basic and common. On the other hand, there are others who think they are Albert Einstein or Isaac Newton and end up choosing overly complicated investigations (often related to Astrophysics). This can absolutely ***backfire*** once you conduct your experiments, eventually leading to an IA that makes no sense at all. In conclusion, don't choose a very simple or a very complicated topic. Then what should you choose? Let's start with some IA topics that often leads to poor grades and creates a negative impression on the examiner's mind.

If you are aiming for a top grade, I wouldn't recommend basing your IA on the following:

1. Projectile motion
2. Simple Pendulum experiments
3. Effect of temperature on elasticity
4. Using computer simulation to determine the charge of an electron
5. Investigating the gauss magnetic gun
6. Exploring Hooke's law for a rubber band
7. Topics related to astrophysics (Don't be too ambitious!)
8. Resonance of a music string
9. Measuring electrical resistance of a putty
10. Database labs
11. Effect of mass on inertia

These topics are either so common that they make it difficult to show original, critical thinking or are overly complicated in a way that loses focus on the experiment. For all of these topics, you would need considerable **extra work** and an extremely high-quality final product to score a good '7'.

Let's not take any risks and keep the following 2 steps in mind when choosing our IA topic:

- When you choose a topic, think of the **relationship between the independent and dependent variable**. If your topic is good, the relationship should not be obvious. For example, let's consider the topic 'Length vs Time Period for a Simple Pendulum'. The moment I look at the topic, I already know that an increase in length of the string leads to an increase in the time period. It therefore isn't a worthy topic to investigate as the conclusions of the experiment is obvious before conducting the investigation. The whole point of the Physics IA is 'exploration'. Explore a physics concept that you are unfamiliar with. Therefore, choose your topic wisely.
- Don't do topics where the independent or dependent variable is not explicitly clear. These are most common in astrophysics-based topics as carrying out the experiment is virtually impossible (you are not a scientist yet). Choose practical topics. You should be able to conduct the experiment in your school lab and you should have all the necessary apparatus to do so. Don't be overambitious. Keep the experiment simple and leave the complicated work to the analysis section.

Let's revisit the (ineffective) topic: 'Length vs Time Period for a Simple Pendulum'. You can pick a simple topic and try making it more interesting. For example, what if I use a torsional pendulum instead of a simple pendulum. All of a sudden, the topic looks a little more intriguing.

'Length vs Time Period for a Torsional Pendulum'. Wow. A small change in the type of pendulum leaves much more room for analysis that the examiner doesn't see often. It lets you explore a new type of pendulum that **you** are unaware about. Thus, if you are unable to come up with your own topic, pick a basic topic and modify it into an interesting one. Don't directly lift topics from online as many people will do that. Take those topics and modify it, make it intriguing. Show genuine interest.

Demonstrating Personal Engagement

You might argue that the personal engagement component has only 2 marks, why care about it? But you must understand that your personal engagement plays a large role in creating an impression of your entire IA on the examiner's mind. A common misconception is that personal engagement is assessed based on your introduction paragraph. Some people write ridiculous statements in their introduction such as 'I have always wanted to explore this topic from my childhood' or make up awful reasons to fake their personal engagement thinking they have easily earned the 2 marks. Don't cheat yourself! Nobody is going to give you any marks for exaggerated statements. It actually shows a lack of understanding of what personal engagement it!

In fact, personal engagement is assessed holistically, not just in your first two paragraphs. Let's break this component down. The following demonstrates genuine personal engagement:

- Creative and original topics: choose riveting topics that have no obvious conclusions
- Detailed analysis and not shying away from challenges
- Deep understanding of the scientific principles involved
- Showing dedication to your research by demonstrating creative thinking
- Connecting your investigation to the real world (this is very important as it demonstrates the significance of your investigation) and carrying out a competent investigation rather than fitting it into a pre-existing template

Hence, please avoid over-emphasizing personal significance by writing artificial comments about your interests. An interest in the general topic is not enough for earning these 2 marks. Demonstrate personal engagement in your research question, analysis and methodology. Don't add a section in your IA called 'personal engagement' and make a fool out of yourself.

Exploration

The following points are used in the evaluation of the exploration component in your IA:

- **Well-defined independent and dependent variable**: Make sure your variables are quantifiable (we don't want bar graphs!). Make sure your investigation clearly has **one** independent and **one** dependent variable. Investigating multiple independent or dependent variables will not add any value to your IA.
- Describing **scientific concepts relevant** to your investigation: A good IA topic always has a scientific principle associated with it or involves the calculation of an important scientific constant. In your introduction, rather than wasting space faking your interest in the topic, describe the scientific principle behind your topic and demonstrate understanding of that concept possibly with the aid of a diagram (diagrams provide a great impression!). If your topic doesn't have an underlying physics principle, it is time to discard it and choose a new one
- Showing awareness of **safety, ethical, environmental concerns** regarding your topic: Make sure you include at least one safety concern and solution. Examiners really look out for this as this makes your research more professional and demonstrates your awareness. If you feel your experiment doesn't have any such concerns, think harder! It must have a safety issue. Even if the only risk is apparatus falling on your feet or water spilling onto the floor. These are valid (though quite trivial!) safety concerns. I recommend you include at least one.

- Clear and **intricate methodology**: Make sure your IA has a good half a page dedicated to methodology where you write down every step of your experiment. Include all the apparatus and associated uncertainties without fail. Make your methodology as unconventional (examiners don't like traditional methodologies) and interesting as possible, without compromising on reliability. It should tell the examiners that you were willing to try new things out and not shy away from challenges.
- **Real world application**: The more your topic is relevant to the real world, the better it is. This criterion is not only essential for exploration but also for personal engagement. Make sure you include a paragraph in your introduction where you describe the connection between your topic and the real world. Answer the question, 'Why is your topic so important or significant?'

Finally, remember that this component of your IA is probably the most important for the IA's overall success. Follow the above points closely and you should be fine. The key point in this component is that you should be able to understand the underlying physics concept behind your investigation and demonstrate it clearly in great depth and detail.

Analysis

This component is extremely important and assesses the following points:

- Errors and uncertainties
- Data collection and processing
- Graphing (most important)
- Scope of data
- Example calculations

While the above points might seem fairly straightforward on first sight, they aren't. But I promise you that if you follow these simple steps, you will score good marks in the analysis section:

- Make sure the column headings in your tables includes quantity, unit and uncertainty with unit
- Don't make your graph look over-complicated. It should be readable
- Use the **appropriate keywords** in your analysis of the graph (students often get confused between 'linear' and 'proportional' so watch out!)
- **Appreciate what your data does** and conduct an analysis appropriate to your investigation. Don't do any unnecessary analysis just to fill the space. Draw a maximum and minimum gradient only when necessary for example. Another example is to make sure the shape of your graph is appropriate. Just because it supports your conclusions, doesn't mean you can fit a linear graph when your data

scatter suggests a clear curve. (Note: your result doesn't need to be perfectly matching the literature data. Even if your investigation results are slightly incorrect and differ from the actual data, no problem! You can justify this in your evaluation section. Nobody expects perfection!).

- Make sure the **number of significant figures** for your data values and uncertainties are appropriate. You can read the first chapter of the IB Physics HL Cambridge textbook to understand more about significant figures and general rules regarding significant figures and uncertainties in general. Please read the chapter thoroughly before doing your IA to make sure your uncertainty processing is correct
- **Focus on physics, not math!** This is not a math IA. The examiners don't expect you to do complex math in your analysis section and doing that will not earn you extra credit. Your focus should always be on physics. Connect your mathematical error analysis with the underlying physics concepts. Often, make references to the physical meaning of your data, not just mathematical. This is a physics IA!
- Make sure your graph includes all the elements it needs to such as axis, uncertainties, axis units, error bars (horizontal not necessary but vertical error bars are a must), data points and an appropriate graph line. Check if your graph really has a zero origin and don't artificially fit it into what you want it to be. If your graph is supposed to start from the origin but your data doesn't support, it probably means your experiment has systematic errors. This can be a great asset in the evaluation section

Read your IA at least 5 times and make sure you have covered all the elements that are needed for a comprehensive analysis. Include example calculations for each data processing and show the examiner your understanding. Don't ever assume that the examiner will infer what you have done on his own. Mention all the steps.

Evaluation

By the time you do this section, you are probably quite exhausted. This is why so many students find this component really annoying. It is nearly impossible to get full marks in this component but getting 5 out of 6 is possible. The following are some simple strategies that will help you earn maximum marks:

- Demonstrate an understanding of Physics. This is the most important point, and most students forget this. You are not expected to just state whether your experiment satisfies the research question or not but explain the connection between the conclusion of your results and the actual scientific theory. Make sure you give **physical meaning to the results** and processed uncertainties, not just mathematical. Explain the underlying physics concept in good depth.

A great evaluation you can do is taking the equation for your processed experiment graph and combining it with a theoretical equation that predicts the graph and uses a physics constant (for example, maybe your theoretical equation uses g). You can then substitute your processed results to try and generate a value for this constant. While this is a complicated process, it provides a **quantifiable measure** of the accuracy of your experiment.

- When stating your experimental errors, divide them into systematic and random errors. Explain three items: Source of error, significance of error and practical improvements. **[Very important]** When mentioning the source of error clearly explain how that error affects your experimental conclusions. In the significance section, answer the question 'why is that error significant?'. In the improvement section, mention what the improvement is and how will it improve the accuracy of the conclusion. Always link your points to the **effect on the conclusion**
- Make sure you include strengths of your investigation as well. Don't just mention weaknesses

Yes, the evaluation section is tricky and full marks can't be guaranteed. But if you follow the above points closely, you should be able to easily earn your 5 out of 6 marks. I recommend including at least 5 systematic and random errors in a table form with three columns (source of error, significance, and improvements). Make sure your errors are not just human errors (such as parallax) and include other significant errors in equipment and methodology as well. Moreover, include at least 2 strengths as they are equally important. Finally, make sure you include a final paragraph in your IA with the heading 'Future research' where you describe an extension to your current investigation (potential topics that can be researched in the future).

Communication

This is one of the slightly easier components and definitely scoring as far as you follow the following steps:

- Make sure your research is **focused on the research question** and doesn't include unnecessary historical background or fake interest. Your focus should be on physics.
- Don't include a title page or a table of contents. However, include your research question and a short descriptive title at the start of your research report.
- **Referencing** is extremely important. Make sure you reference any images taken from the internet or any other scientific work of others. Eliminate the probability of possible plagiarism
- Don't exceed the **12-page limit**. The 12 pages includes your bibliography, which should not be more than half a page. I would recommend font size 12, Times New Roman with 1.15 line spacing but that is up to you. If you exceed page limit, you will be penalized under Communication

Remember that this component just like personal engagement is assessed holistically and not based on a paragraph or two. Make sure your references are not from artificial sources as this can lead to demerit points.

Checklist

Now that I have covered all the pointers, I would like to reinforce the very important ones in the form of a checklist. Please follow this checklist and make sure you have all the points ticked.

Does your IA include	Yes or No
1. A descriptive title and research question at the start of the IA?	
2. An intro that addresses the physics principle associated behind the topic?	
3. A paragraph dedicated for the connection between your topic and real-world application?	
4. A hypothesis? (Highly recommended although not needed)	
5. Independent, Dependent and Control Variables? (At least 5 control variables)	
6. Apparatus (with uncertainty of each instrument)?	
7. Methodology?	
8. Experimental set-up (preferably a picture)?	
9. Safety concerns (safety, environmental and ethical)?	
10. Qualitative and Quantitative observations?	
11. Processed data and data processing?	
12. Experimental error calculations?	
13. Experimental uncertainty propagation?	
14. Graphical presentation?	
15. Well-formed Conclusion (with connection between results and theory)?	
16. Strengths of your investigation?	
17. Weaknesses of your investigation?	
18. Source of Error, significance, and improvements?	
19. Random errors and Systematic errors in the evaluation section?	
20. Extension or future research?	

Moreover, make sure your IA addresses the 5 important questions mentioned below. These are fundamental questions that must be satisfied if you want a 6 or 7 in your IA.

1. Have you appreciated well-known physics theories in your IA report?
2. Does your research question have a clearly defined independent and dependent variable (only one each)?
3. Are all your images and scientific work references clearly referenced?
4. Have you often highlighted a physical meaning to your experimental data?
5. Does your topic have a real-world application?

Sample Level ‘7’ IA

Below is a sample Physics IA (which scored 22 out of 24) that will give you a good idea of how to write a ‘7’ quality IA.

Note: The IA is by no means ‘perfect’ and can be improved. Your task: Spot the improvements and note them down!

Task

Read the IA that begins on the next page and write down 4 strengths, weaknesses, and potential improvements that you have identified in the below table. This exercise will help you spot valuable points that you can then incorporate in your IA!

Strengths	Weaknesses	Improvements

[SAMPLE] Physics Level '7' Internal Assessment

1: Research question

How accurately can we measure the shear modulus of a cast steel wire by measuring period of disk rotation for varying suspension lengths (0.05 m, 0.10 m, 0.15 m, 0.20 m, 0.25 m, 0.30 m, 0.35 m, 0.40 m, 0.45 m and 0.50 m) of a torsion pendulum?

2: Introduction

2.1: Rationale

Having this ornamental at the same time unorthodox and old-fashioned torsion clock at home, I was intrigued by its mechanism and learnt that it keeps time with an aid of a torsion pendulum, a type of pendulum that rotates about the vertical axis of the wire and oscillates clockwise and anticlockwise rather than swinging like a conventional pendulum. This led me to study these torsional pendulums and their mechanism in detail and during my riveting exploration, I realized that these pendulums, though seem trivial on first sight, play a fairly salient role in this modern and industrialized society. The discipline of engineering makes use of scientific principles to design and construct machines, structures and other crucial items including bridges, tunnels, roads, buildings and so on. The construction of all these items depends on the calculation of an important constant, the shear modulus, also referred to as the rigidity modulus. This shear modulus is the ratio of shear stress to shear strain and is a measure of the stiffness of a material[1], which informs civil and mechanical engineers when a structural implant will deform. It was quite intriguing to realize that such a simple torsional pendulum that operates a torsion clock can also be used to determine such a cardinal constant in the field of engineering, making it all the more significant. This major application of torsional pendulum led me to ponder how accurately can we calculate the shear modulus of a steel wire with the aid of a simple torsion pendulum. This very curiosity of thought and genuine interest led me to undertake this investigation with the research question, 'How accurately can we measure the shear modulus of a cast steel wire by measuring period of disk rotation for varying suspension lengths of a torsion pendulum?'

2.2: Background information

1 Helmenstine, Anne Marie. "How the Shear Modulus Describes Material Rigidity." *ThoughtCo*, ThoughtCo, 30 Jan. 2019, www.thoughtco.com/shear-modulus-4176406.

Figure 1: An annotated image showing a torsional disk

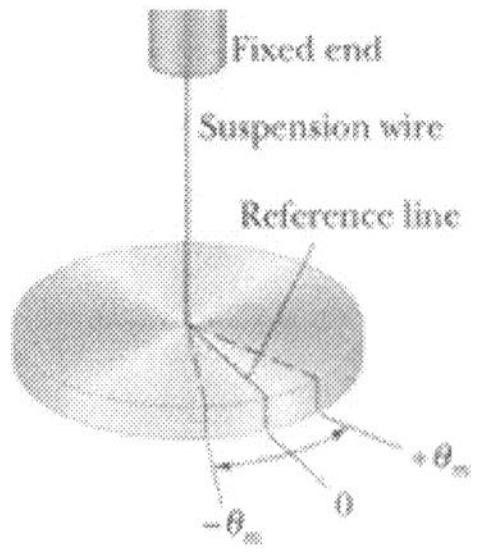

Torque is the measure of the amount of force required for an object to rotate[2]. When the torsional pendulum is rotated anti-clockwise, for instance, the wire will also rotate and the stiffness in the wire will cause the wire to exert a clockwise restoring torque on the disc. This restoring torque brings back the pendulum to equilibrium position.

These torsion pendulums, other than aiding operation of torsion clocks and determination of shear modulus, have several other practical applications in this real world such as helping discern the frictional forces between solid surfaces and liquid environments, characteristic properties of polymers and so on, making them important devices.

On the other hand, shear modulus, which is also known as rigidity modulus, is the ratio of shear stress to shear strain. A large shear modulus value indicates high rigidity, and a large magnitude of force is required to produce deformation. On the contrary, a small shear modulus is an indicator of softness where less force is required to produce deformation. The determination of this value is integral because items such as aircraft carriers, prosthetic limbs, bridges, skyscrapers, and artificial joints[3], all require very high strength materials to stay stable. If the limit is exceeded, then it is highly probable that the whole structure will collapse. So, the magnitude of shear modulus can be used to estimate when the material is going to collapse and accordingly, actions can be taken to prevent such a mishap. This constant has further real-world applications as it helps analyse the responsiveness of a material due to strain variation[4] and effectively identifies the elastic material of a material due to shear loading, making it very significant in solving various engineering problems.

2.3: Derivation for the effect of suspension length on the period of a torsional pendulum

---

2 "Torque (Article)." *Khan Academy*, Khan Academy, www.khanacademy.org/science/physics/torque-angular-momentum/torque-tutorial/a/torque.

3 Gemma, Davis. "Uses of Young's Modulus." *Prezi.com*, Jan. 2015, prezi.com/4dgmqlffg7jv/uses-of-youngs-modulus/.

4 "Chegg.com." *Definition of Shear Modulus | Chegg.com*, www.chegg.com/homework-help/definitions/shear-modulus-8.

Let c be the coefficient of stiffness (torsional constant), θ be the angle of rotation, τ be the restoring torque and I be the moment of inertia of the disk

Moment of inertia of the disk which is oscillating perpendicular to its face through the centre,

$$I = \frac{1}{2} \times M \times R^2$$

where M is the mass of the disk and R is the radius of the disk

When the disk is rotated from equilibrium position with an angle θ, the restoring torque,

$$\tau = -c \times \theta$$

Rate of change of angular velocity (angular acceleration),

$$\alpha = \frac{-c \times \theta}{I} \qquad (1.1)$$

where I is the moment of inertia of the disk

For simple harmonic motion, angular acceleration,

$$\alpha = x \times -\omega^2 \qquad (1.2)$$

where ω is the angular frequency and x is the displacement

Equating equations (1.1) and (1.2) yields,

$$\omega = \sqrt{\frac{c}{I}}$$

Time taken for one oscillation (time period),

$$T = \frac{2\pi}{\omega} = 2\pi \times \sqrt{\frac{I}{c}} \qquad (1.3)$$

Coefficient of stiffness,

$$c = \frac{1}{2} \times \frac{\pi \times n \times r^4}{l} \qquad (1.4)$$

where r is the radius of suspension wire, n is the rigidity modulus of suspension wire and l is the length of the suspension wire

Substituting the value of c from (1.4) in (1.3) and then squaring both sides of the equation will yield,

$$n = \frac{8\pi Il}{r^4T^2}$$

Thus, with a purpose of investigating the application of torsion pendulum in calculating this constant, I have decided to conduct an experiment in which I will be constructing a simple torsional pendulum and measuring the period of disk rotation, using a stopwatch, at various suspension lengths: 0.05 m, 0.10 m, 0.15 m, 0.20 m, 0.25 m, 0.30 m, 0.35 m, 0.40 m, 0.45 m and 0.50 m. The aim of this experiment is to calculate the value of rigidity modulus (n) of the steel suspension wire as accurately as possible.

3: Hypothesis

$$n = \frac{8\pi Il}{r^4T^2}$$

Taking the above equation into consideration, this experiment hypothesizes a linear relationship between the time period of disk rotation and suspension length. Graph between length of suspension wire and square of period of disk rotation is expected to pass through the origin (0,0). In order to achieve such a linear relationship, other factors in the formula like mass of disk, radius of steel wire, and radius of disk must be kept constant.

4: Experimental design

4.1: Variables

4.1.1: Independent variable

The independent variable in this experiment is the length of steel suspension wire, which was measured using a ruler (±0.05cm). A total of 10 different suspension lengths were used: 0.05 m, 0.10 m, 0.15 m, 0.20 m, 0.25 m, 0.30 m, 0.35 m, 0.40 m, 0.45 m and 0.50 m. 10 different lengths were chosen since it is believed that having more independent variable values would increase the number of data samples on the graph, which will cause trends and patterns to form more easily and lead to more reliable deductions. Similarly, 10 trials were carried out for each length of suspension wire to ensure accurate and reliable data, with minimum random error.

4.1.2: Dependent variable

The dependent variable in this experiment is the time period of one disk oscillation, which was measured with an aid of a stopwatch (±0.01s). Time taken for 10 oscillations was measured and then time period was calculated. This helped improve the reliability of the results obtained since the probability of systematic error due to human reaction time was reduced.

4.1.3: Control variable

Variable controlled	How is the variable controlled?	Reason for controlling
1. Moment of Inertia of disk	The same disk was used in each trial so that the mass and radius of the disk were kept constant	In any experiment, at most 1 variable can be altered and since length is the independent variable of this experiment, other variables that affect the calculation of shear modulus such as the moment of inertia of disk needs to be kept constant
2. Angular rotation of disk	The protractor was used as a reference point to ensure that the disk was released from the same angle each trial	By making sure that the angular rotation of the disk is constant each trial, fair experimentation is ensured since length of suspension wire is the only variable altered
3. Material and radius of string	The same steel string was used in each trial	By using the same string every time, fair experimentation is ensured since length of suspension wire is the only variable altered
4. Wind conditions	The experiment was carried out in an airconditioned, closed area without any windows and doors, leaving no room for wind to affect the experiment	A gust of air can affect the period of disk rotation by altering the disk's motion, which can lead to unreliable results
5. Tilt of string	The string was kept perpendicular to the floor surface almost always	While swinging, slight tilt of string might affect the motion of disk rotation, which can affect the time period

4.2: Apparatus

1. Suspension wire made of steel
2. A disk of mass 600 g (±0.01g) and radius 7.0 cm (±0.05cm)
3. A wooden ruler (±0.05cm) used to measure length of suspension wire and radius of disk
4. A wooden protractor used as a reference point for measuring angle of rotation
5. Retort stand apparatus for holding the suspension wire tightly
6. Thread which aided measurement of different suspension lengths
7. Stopwatch (±0.01s) for measuring time period of 10 oscillations
8. Electronic mass balance for measuring mass of disk (±0.01g)
9. Micrometer screw gauge for measuring radius of suspension wire (0.950mm) (±0.005mm)

4.3: Experimental set-up

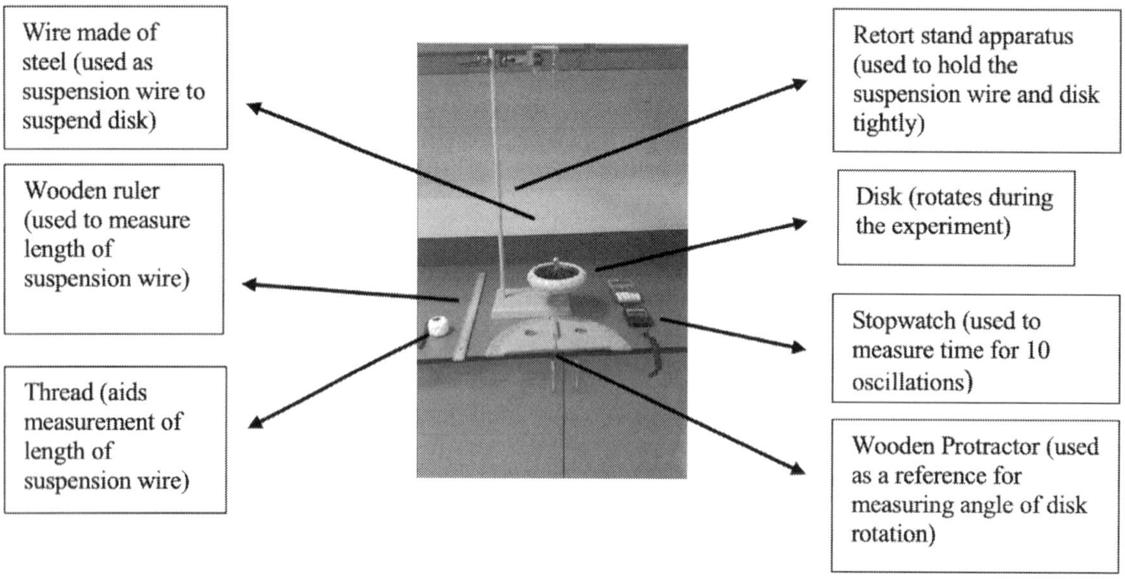

4.4: Procedure

1. A circular disk was taken, and its mass and radius were measured using an electronic mass balance and meter rule respectively (mass: 600 g (±0.01g) and radius: 7.0 cm (±0.05cm))
2. Next, a steel wire was taken, and its radius was measured using a micrometer screw gauge (±0.005mm)
3. Then, a torsional pendulum was constructed by inserting the steel suspension wire into the circular disk and the apparatus was fitted into a retort stand
4. The length of the suspension wire was adjusted by inserting the wire into the circular disk and a 0.05 m suspension wire length, measured using the meter rule (±0.05cm) with the aid of a thread, was ensured
5. The disk was kept motionless, in equilibrium position prior to the start of experiment
6. A mark was made on the circular disk using a pen and the disk was rotated 180° in clockwise direction, keeping the protractor as reference for measuring the rotation angle
7. The disk was released as such without exerting any external force and immediately a stopwatch was started
8. The time taken for 10 disk oscillations was measured and the stopwatch (±0.01s) was stopped after the tenth disk oscillation, keeping the pen mark as a reference for precisely stopping the stopwatch at the right instant
9. Steps 5 to 7 were repeated using suspension lengths 0.10 m, 0.15 m, 0.20 m, 0.25 m, 0.30 m, 0.35 m, 0.40 m, 0.45 m and 0.50 m and 10 trials were carried out in each experiment
10. Finally, the time taken for 1 disk oscillation was calculated by dividing the time taken for 10 disk oscillations by the number of oscillations

4.5: Safety consideration

Hazard	Measure taken to reduce	Consequence (1-5)	Likelihood (1-5)
1. Torsion pendulum falling off the edge of table and breaking which can cause potential injury to the leg	As a precaution, safety shoes should be worn, and apparatus should not be kept near the edge of the table	2 (minor)	3 (possible)

[Consequence: 1 (negligible), 2 (minor), 3 (moderate), 4 (major), 5 (catastrophic)

Likelihood: 1 (rare), 2 (unlikely), 3 (possible), 4 (likely), 5 (almost certain)5]

There are no environmental or ethical issues associated with this experiment.

5: Raw data

5.1: Qualitative observations

As the suspension length increased, the magnitude of disk rotation visibly increased as the pen mark on the disk was rotated to a greater degree. The disk took more time to oscillate. When suspension length was less, the magnitude of disk rotation visibly decreased and the pen mark on the disk was rotated to a much less degree. Each rotation took less time and as a result, the calculated time period is less.

5.2: Quantitative observations

Raw Table 1: A table (an excel screenshot) depicting the time taken for 10 disk oscillations for the corresponding suspension lengths of the steel wire (Anomalous data has been struck off)

Length/cm (±0.05 cm)	Time taken for 10 oscillations/s (±0.01 s)									
	Trial 1	Trial 2	Trial 3	Trial 4	Trial 5	Trial 6	Trial 7	Trial 8	Trial 9	Trial 10
5.00	15.57	15.81	15.75	16.03	15.84	14.96	15.61	16.26	15.09	15.34
10.00	21.19	~~24.37~~	21.44	21.03	21.35	21.32	21.56	22.07	21.33	21.94
15.00	25.56	26.16	25.71	25.72	25.72	25.89	26.11	25.36	25.98	25.47
20.00	29.31	29.28	29.43	29.22	29.38	29.24	29.99	30.13	29.03	29.56
25.00	32.91	33.16	33.29	33.07	33.38	33.45	34.03	33.56	33.40	33.10
30.00	35.57	35.97	35.94	35.97	37.03	35.87	35.97	36.08	35.23	35.12
35.00	39.00	39.13	38.68	38.52	39.15	38.75	38.90	39.01	38.56	39.32
40.00	40.97	40.85	40.96	40.81	40.82	40.76	40.69	40.92	~~43.87~~	41.00
45.00	44.06	43.63	43.86	43.52	44.05	43.57	43.68	44.02	43.50	43.94
50.00	46.34	46.46	46.12	47.02	46.13	46.38	46.90	46.35	46.48	46.22

5 *Risk Assessment Scoring and Matrix* , http://www.cardiffandvaleuhb.wales.nhs.uk/sitesplus/documents/1143/Appendix 21.pdf.

6: Processed data

6.1: Processed quantitative observations

Processed table 1: A table (an excel screenshot) displaying the average time taken for 10 oscillations, 1 oscillation and the square of average time period of disk rotation for different suspension lengths

Length/cm (±0.05 cm)	Average Time taken for 10 oscillations/s	Average Time taken for 1 oscillation/s	(Average Time taken for one oscillation)²/s²
5.00	15.63	1.563	2.44
10.00	21.47	2.147	4.63
15.00	25.77	2.577	6.64
20.00	29.46	2.946	8.68
25.00	33.34	3.334	11.11
30.00	35.88	3.588	12.87
35.00	38.90	3.890	15.13
40.00	40.86	4.086	16.70
45.00	43.78	4.378	19.17
50.00	46.44	4.644	21.57

Processed table 2: A table displaying the uncertainties of average time taken for 10 oscillations, 1 oscillation and the square of average time period of disk rotation for different suspension lengths

Length/cm (±0.05 cm)	Uncertainty of average time taken for 10 oscillations/±	Uncertainty of average time taken for 1 oscillation/±	Uncertainty of (Average Time taken for one oscillation)²/±
5.00	0.65	0.065	0.20
10.00	0.52	0.052	0.22
15.00	0.40	0.040	0.21
20.00	0.55	0.055	0.32
25.00	0.56	0.056	0.37
30.00	0.96	0.096	0.68
35.00	0.40	0.040	0.31
40.00	0.16	0.016	0.13
45.00	0.28	0.028	0.25
50.00	0.45	0.045	0.42

6.2: Data processing

The following example calculations are for suspension length = 5 cm

Example calculation 1: calculation of average time taken for 10 oscillations

Average time taken for 10 oscillations =

$$\frac{15.57 + 15.81 + 15.75 + 16.03 + 15.84 + 14.96 + 15.61 + 16.26 + 15.09 + 15.34}{10} = 15.63\ s$$

Example calculation 2: calculation of average time taken for one oscillation (average time period)

$$\text{Average time period} = \frac{Average\ time\ taken\ for\ 10\ oscillations}{10} = \frac{15.63}{10} = 1.563\ \text{s}$$

Example calculation 3: calculation of square of average time taken for one oscillation (average time period)

$(\text{Average Time taken for one oscillation})^2 = (1.56)^2 = 2.44\ s^2$

6.3: Experimental error calculations

6.3.1: Propagation of random error due to instruments

Sample calculation for stopwatch (maximum uncertainty):

$$\frac{Uncertainty}{Maximum\ Amount} \times 100 = \frac{0.01}{47.02} \times 100 = 0.021\ \%$$

Sample calculation for total percentage error for stopwatch: maximum percentage uncertainty + minimum percentage uncertainty = 0.067 + 0.021 = 0.088 %

Processed table 3: A table showing the total percentage random error calculated using all the instruments

Instrument	Uncertainty (±)	Minimum uncertainty/%	Maximum uncertainty/%	Percentage (%)
Micrometer screw gauge	±0.005 mm	0.526		0.526
Stopwatch	±0.01 s	0.067	0.021	0.088
Wooden ruler	±0.5 mm	1.0	0.1	1.100
Mass balance	±0.01 g	0.0017		0.0017
Total uncertainty =				1.720 %

Hence, the total percentage random error of this experiment due to instrumentation is 1.720 %

6.3.2: Experimental uncertainty propagation

The following example calculations are for suspension length = 5 cm

Example calculation 1: calculation of uncertainty of average time for 10 oscillations

$$\Delta T_{10\ oscillations}, \text{ where } T \text{ is the average time taken for } 10 \text{ oscillations} = \frac{T_{max} - T_{min}}{2}$$

$$\text{Estimate of uncertainty of the quantity} = \frac{16.26 - 14.96}{2} = \pm 0.65 \text{ s}$$

Example calculation 2: calculation of uncertainty of average time taken for 1 oscillation

$$\Delta T_{1\ oscillation}, \text{ where } T \text{ is average time for 1 oscillation} = \frac{\Delta T_{10\ oscillations}}{10} = \frac{0.65}{10} = \pm 0.065 \text{ s}$$

Example calculation 3: calculation of uncertainty of (average time taken for 1 oscillation)²

$$\Delta T^2, \text{ where } T \text{ is the average time taken for 1 oscillation} = 2 \times \frac{\Delta T_{1\ oscillation}}{T_{1\ oscillation}} \times T^2$$

$$= 2 \times \frac{0.065}{1.56} \times 2.44 = \pm 0.20\ s^2$$

7: Data analysis

7.1: Graphical presentation

Graph 1: A graph displaying the relationship between suspension length and time period of disk rotation for a torsional pendulum

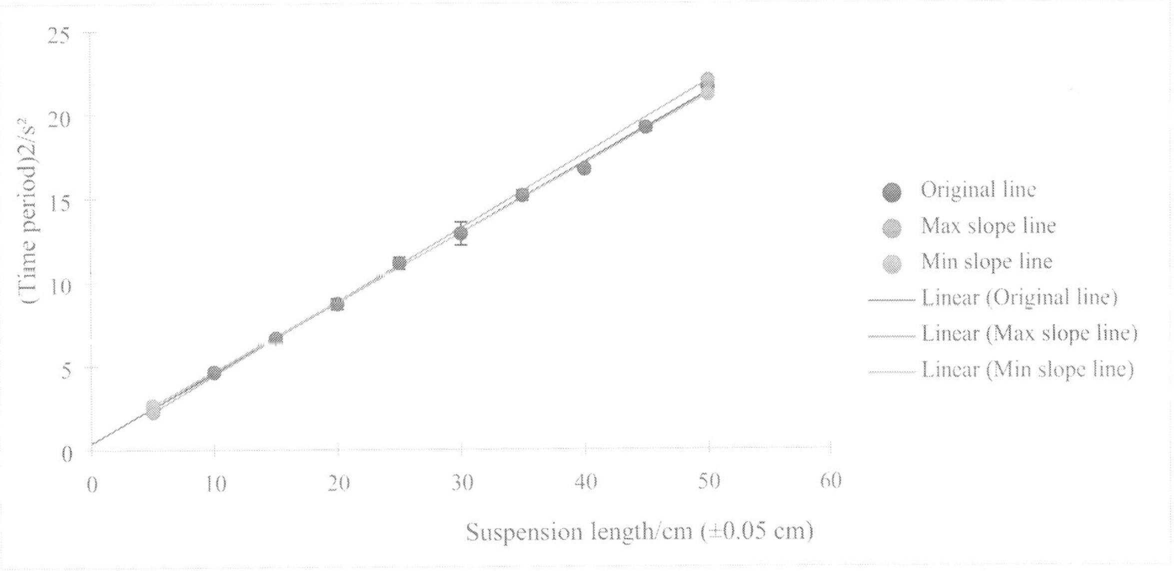

7.2: Calculation of rigidity modulus

The gradient of graph 1 $= \frac{y2 - y1}{x2 - x1} = \frac{2.44 - 19.17}{5 - 45} = 0.418$ $(\pm 0.014\, s^2cm^{-1})$

Moment of inertia, I $= \frac{1}{2} \times M \times R^2$ (M is the mass of disk and R is the radius of disk)

$= \frac{1}{2} \times 0.6 \times (0.07)^2 = 0.00147$ kgm² $(\pm 0.00027\, kgm^2)$

$$Rigidity\ modulus, n = \frac{8\pi Il}{r^4T^2} = \frac{8\pi}{r^4} \times \frac{1}{2} \times M \times R^2 \times \frac{l}{T^2} = \frac{8\pi}{(0.00095)^4} \times 0.00147 \times \frac{1}{0.418}$$

$$= 1.085 \times 10^{11}Pa(\pm 21.3 \times 10^9 Pa) = 108.5GPa(\pm 21.3GPa)$$

7.3: Propagation of uncertainties in the calculation of rigidity modulus

Uncertainty in gradient (m) =

$$\frac{Maximum\ gradient - Minimum\ gradient}{2} = \frac{0.4389 - 0.4113}{2} = \pm 0.014$$

$$\frac{\Delta\left(\frac{1}{m}\right)}{\frac{1}{m}} = \frac{\Delta m}{m}; Uncertainty\ in\ the\ inverse\ of\ gradient\left(\Delta\left(\frac{1}{m}\right)\right) = \frac{0.014}{0.418} \times \frac{1}{0.418} = \pm 0.080$$

Uncertainty in moment of inertia,

$$\frac{\Delta I}{I} = \frac{\Delta M}{M} + 2 \times \frac{\Delta R}{R}; \Delta I = \left(\frac{0.1}{0.6} + 2 \times \frac{0.5}{70}\right) \times 0.00147 = \pm 0.00027\, kgm^2$$

Uncertainty in rigidity modulus,

$$\frac{\Delta n}{n} = \frac{\Delta I}{I} + 4 \times \frac{\Delta r}{r} + \Delta\left(\frac{1}{gradient}\right); \Delta n = \frac{0.00027}{0.00147} + 4 \times \frac{0.005}{0.00095} + 0.080 = \pm 21.3\, GPa$$

8: Conclusion

The accuracy of the calculated rigidity modulus depends on the accuracy of the graph of suspension length vs time period since the formula for finding rigidity modulus involves the calculation of $\frac{L}{T^2}$, which is $\frac{1}{m}$, where m is the gradient of the graph of suspension length vs time period. When looking at the context of data and methodology, it is fairly clear from the graph that there is a direct positive correlation between suspension length and time period. A linear relationship (or linear association) is a statistical term used to describe a straight-line relationship between a variable and a constant[6]. There are 2 key evidences in the graph and

6 Hayes, Adam. "Understanding Linear Relationships." *Investopedia*, Investopedia, 6 Jan. 2020,

the data table to suggest a strong positive correlation and linear relation between suspension length and time period, which effectively strengthens the research hypothesis.

1. One key evidence from graph 1 that suggests a linear relationship between suspension length and time period is the equation of the graph ($y = 0.4186x + 0.382$) which takes the form $y = mx + c$, suggesting that the graph is a straight line with a constant gradient
2. The data points plotted on the graph indicate a strong positive correlation. In graph 1, the straight line passes through all but 2 data points (when suspension length = 25 cm and 40 cm). These two data points lie very close to the graph, suggesting strong positive correlation

Furthermore, there are two more important aspects to consider. Firstly, the straight line graph intersects the y-axis at 0.382 and not 0 which is a clear indication that the graph doesn't pass through the origin. This is an evidence for systematic shift in the graph, which could have been caused by a significant systematic error in the experiment. Secondly, error bars on graph 1 are quite significant. It is quite surprising to find error bars appear negligible in most data points as error bars are only significantly visible when the suspension length equals 25 cm and 30 cm. At other suspension lengths, error bars are barely visible or invisible. Among the ones visible, the vertical error bar is most significant when suspension length is 30 cm and has a value of ±0.68. The presence of negligible error bars is evidence for high precision in the data obtained. There is a possible anomaly when suspension length = 40 cm as the line barely passes through it and this slightly weakens the hypothesis, but there is an overall strong support for the hypothesis.

Next, directly addressing the research question, the accuracy of the calculated value for rigidity modulus will be found. 78×10^9 is the literature value of rigidity modulus of cast steel material[7]. Now, the percentage difference between the measured value and literature value will be calculated.

$$\frac{1.085 \times 10^{11} - 78 \times 10^9}{78 \times 10^9} \times 100 = 39.1\%$$

Hence, the percentage error in this experiment is 39.1%.

$$Percentage\ uncertainty = \frac{\Delta n}{n} \times 100 = \frac{21.3}{108.5} \times 100 = 19.6\%$$

---

www.investopedia.com/terms/l/linearrelationship.asp.

7 Engineering ToolBox, (2005). Modulus of Rigidity. [online] Available at: https://www.engineeringtoolbox.com/modulus-rigidity-d_946.html

Since the percentage difference is greater than percentage uncertainty, it is clear that random error alone is not responsible for the difference, hence systematic error is also present. The presence of systematic error is also evidenced by the systematic shift in the graph as y-intercept is 0.382. Moreover, the literature value (78×10^9) lies just outside the range of the calculated value $1.085 \times 10^{11}\ Pa\ (\pm 21.3\ \times 10^9\ Pa)$, which is mostly due to systematic and random errors in the experiment. The use of torsion pendulum to measure the rigidity modulus of a material accurately is becoming increasingly common in this world and this is evinced by the various research being carried out. One such example is the development of a modified torsion pendulum apparatus for measuring the shear modulus of single filaments with uniform micro-sized diameter. In this research, the shear modulus of three types of filaments were accurately found: carbon fibres, copper wires, tungsten wires[8]. Moreover, an accurate calculation of shear modulus of dental materials using a modified torsion pendulum is carried out to estimate the materials' resistance to structural deformation, so it is indubitable that torsion pendulums are important devices and aid accurate measurement of shear modulus.

9: Evaluation

9.1: Strengths of the investigation

Since 10 different suspension lengths were used, an abundant data was obtained, which caused patterns and trends in data to emerge and become easily recognizable. There were 10 repetitions carried out. Repetitions are used to reduce random error in the experiment. It is appropriate to assert that the effects of these random errors were largely offset by the large number of repeats carried out in this experiment, which is a strength of this investigation. Additionally, a significant strength of this experiment is due to the low percentage random error (1.26%) contributed by instrumentation, which is an indication of high precision and reliable results. The presence of insignificant error bars also strengthens the precision of data obtained.

8 Liu, Dabiao, et al. "A Modified Torsion Pendulum for Measuring the Shear Modulus of a Single Micro-Sized Filament." *Acta Mechanica Solida Sinica*, vol. 27, no. 3, 2014, pp. 221–233., doi:10.1016/s0894-9166(14)60032-x.

9.2: Limitations and Improvements

Systematic Error

Source of error	Improvements
1. Slight twists and turns in the suspension wire may have caused measurement of length of string to be inaccurate	This is a highly significant error since twists in the string add additional length which is very difficult to measure using a meter rule. The only way to reduce this error is to make use of a string with minimal or no twists and turns
2. Worn out string which can affect oscillation of disk and thus increase the time period	Worn out string can cause the twisting of the disk to be erratic and not smooth, which can result in unreliable oscillations. To reduce this error, the quality of the string should be cross-checked before the experiment and worn-out strings should be replaced
3. Friction of the string and its pivotal anchor point and air resistance which can increase the time period	Air resistance opposing disk motion during disk rotation along with friction of sting and anchor point are significant systematic errors but there is no feasible way to reduce these errors. One way to avoid air resistance is to carry the experiment out in a vacuum chamber but this is infeasible
4. Zero error due to micrometer screw gauge which can lead to an inaccurate calculation of thickness of string	This is a highly significant error and a direct way to reduce this error is to ensure that the zero of the main scale accurately coincides with the zero of the vernier scale
5. Damping effect of a torsion pendulum due to string and disk which can affect the disk rotation, leading to inaccuracy in the calculated time period	Drag force on the string and air resistance on the disk can lead to damping effect, which is a significant error. It is also notable that the amount of damping depends on the moment of inertia of the disk. A way to reduce damping effect caused by disk is to increase the mass of the disk and thus, its moment of inertia. Similarly, using a string with less twists and turns will also lead to a slight reduction in the damping effect

Random error

Source of error	Improvements
1. Uncertainty in micrometer screw gauge and mass balance which can affect calculated value of thickness of string and mass of disk	This random error is insignificant and requires no improvement since the uncertainty in micrometer ($\pm 0.005mm)$ and uncertainty in mass of disk (($\pm 0.01g)$ are low and inaccuracies will not have a major effect on the conclusion
2. Incorrect starting and stopping time of stopwatch which can affect value of time period	This is an example of human reaction error and is highly significant. The only way to reduce this error is to make use of photo-timer, which is a self-timer and will start and stop accurately
3. Precision of micrometer which can cause slight inaccuracy in the obtained value of thickness of string	In order to improve the precision of result obtained from the micrometer screw gauge, the thickness of the wire should be measured from different parts of the steel wire and then an average of the thickness must be found. Repeating readings and finding mean will reduce random error
4. Though angular rotation was a control variable, it was measured only approximately (judging with eye) using protractor as a reference point	This is not a very significant error since both rigidity modulus and moment of inertia are not affected by the angle of rotation. The formula for rigidity modulus and moment of inertia doesn't contain angle of rotation. So, no improvement is required for this source of error
5. Parallax error which can cause incorrect reading of meter rule while measuring length of string	There is no significant improvement to this error other than to read the meter rule reading from a perpendicular angle. Parallax error due to incorrect reading will not have a significant effect on the conclusion

Hence, the improvements proposed to reduce systematic error will improve the accuracy of results, which will reduce the systematic shift in the graph and improve reliability of conclusion since a more accurate value of rigidity modulus can be found. The improvements proposed to reduce random error will result in a more precise set of data and hence, all data points will either lie on the graph or very close to it.

10: Further research

There are two main ways to measure the rigidity modulus of any material using a torsion pendulum. One is to determine rigidity modulus using a torsion pendulum alone, which was conducted in this investigation. Another method is to determine moment of inertia and rigidity modulus of any material using torsion pendulum with identical masses. This second method can be conducted as an extension and can be used to confirm the reliability and accuracy of the results obtained. Another potential extension is to investigate the effect of factors other than suspension length, such as mass of disk, on the time period of disk rotation.

11: Bibliography

1. Engineering Toolbox, (2005). Modulus of Rigidity. [online] Available at: https://www.engineeringtoolbox.com/modulus-rigidity-d_946.html
2. *Risk Assessment Scoring and Matrix* , http://www.cardiffandvaleuhb.wales.nhs.uk/sitesplus/documents/1143/Appendix 21.pdf.
3. Hayes, Adam. "Understanding Linear Relationships." *Investopedia*, Investopedia, 6 Jan. 2020, www.investopedia.com/terms/l/linearrelationship.asp.
4. "Chegg.com." *Definition of Shear Modulus | Chegg.com*, www.chegg.com/homework-help/definitions/shear-modulus-8.
5. Helmenstine, Anne Marie. "How the Shear Modulus Describes Material Rigidity." *ThoughtCo*, ThoughtCo, 30 Jan. 2019, www.thoughtco.com/shear-modulus-4176406.
6. "Torque (Article)." *Khan Academy*, Khan Academy, www.khanacademy.org/science/physics/torque-angular-momentum/torque-tutorial/a/torque.
7. Gemma, Davis. "Uses of Young's Modulus." *Prezi.com*, Jan. 2015, prezi.com/4dgmqlffg7jv/uses-of-youngs-modulus/.
8. vlab.amrita.edu,. (2013). Rigidity Modulus of The Suspension Wire of A Torsion Pendulum. Retrieved 26 January 2020, from vlab.amrita.edu/?sub=1&brch=280&sim=1518&cnt=5
9. xmltwo.ibo.org/publications/DP/Group4/d_4_physi_tsm_1408_1/pdf/update2017/Example05_annotations_en.pdf.
10. Liu, Dabiao, et al. "A Modified Torsion Pendulum for Measuring the Shear Modulus of a Single Micro-Sized Filament." Acta Mechanica Solida Sinica, vol. 27, no. 3, 2014, pp. 221–233., doi:10.1016/s0894-9166(14)60032-x.

Author's Note

This book is the joint effort of 3 IB Graduates (one now studying at UCL in London and two at NUS in Singapore). We worked on these answers for over 6 months during the 2020 lockdown (in place of our May IB exams!), which involved a lot of international skype calls and word-document sharing, not to mention a lot of Physics too.

While we didn't need exams to get our IB Grades (43, 43 and 45), we hope you found this resource useful for your own revision.

If you have any feedback whatsoever, or would like some additional advice for IB Physics revision or coursework, feel free to contact us at:

purplewave.publishing@gmail.com

Do send an email to the above address if you would like a copy of a sample 'A' grade Extended Essay written by a 45-point student (don't worry, it is complimentary, and you do not have to pay anything extra)

If you found this book useful, please do recommend it to your friends. Thanks!

All the best for your exams!

The Purplewave group

Made in the USA
Monee, IL
11 February 2022

91084216R00096